Faith Hounds

Faith Hounds

A Relentless Pursuit

WILLIAM N. MITCHELL

Foreword by David Brown

Illustrated by Amanda Weemes

RESOURCE *Publications* · Eugene, Oregon

FAITH HOUNDS
A Relentless Pursuit

Copyright © 2022 William N. Mitchell. All rights reserved. Except for brief quotations in critical publications or reviews, no part of this book may be reproduced in any manner without prior written permission from the publisher. Write: Permissions, Wipf and Stock Publishers, 199 W. 8th Ave., Suite 3, Eugene, OR 97401.

Resource Publications
An Imprint of Wipf and Stock Publishers
199 W. 8th Ave., Suite 3
Eugene, OR 97401

www.wipfandstock.com

PAPERBACK ISBN: 978-1-6667-3763-9
HARDCOVER ISBN: 978-1-6667-9730-5
EBOOK ISBN: 978-1-6667-9731-2

March 17, 2022 11:24 AM

Scriptures taken from the Holy Bible, New International Version®, NIV®. Copyright © 1973, 1978, 1984, 2011 by Biblica, Inc.™ Used by permission of Zondervan. All rights reserved worldwide. www.zondervan.com The "NIV" and "New International Version" are trademarks registered in the United States Patent and Trademark Office by Biblica, Inc.™

All Scripture quotations, unless otherwise indicated, are taken from the Amplified Bible, Copyright © 2015 by The Lockman Foundation. Used by permission.

Scripture quotations from The Authorized (King James) Version. Rights in the Authorized Version in the United Kingdom are vested in the Crown. Reproduced by permission of the Crown's patentee, Cambridge University Press

Unless otherwise indicated, all Scripture quotations are taken from the Holy Bible, New Living Translation, copyright © 1996, 2004, 2015 by Tyndale House Foundation. Used by permission of Tyndale House Publishers, Carol Stream, Illinois 60188. All rights reserved.

This book is dedicated to my nephew Mytchell. Nephew, you are the living and breathing embodiment of God's faithfulness and the truths this book holds.

Contents

Foreword by DAVID BROWN | ix

A Message from the Author | xi

Acknowledgments | xiii

JESUS IS THE CAKE | 1

FROM THE SPIRIT, THROUGH THE SOUL AND TO THE BODY | 12

PRAYER | 17

OUR REQUEST, HIS WILL | 34

FAITH HOUND . . . THE PURSUIT | 44

THE WAIT AND EXPECTATION | 51

RESTING | 60

DUE SEASON | 71

HINDRANCES | 81

WHAT COMES INSTEAD AND DISAPPOINTMENT | 94

REAL FAITH | 98

UNDER ATTACK | 117

THEN COMES THE *PRIZE* | 133

Bibliography | 137

Foreword

I've watched Will Mitchell grow from a boy into a man. From a normal everyday teenager into a dedicated husband and father. From an ordinary church going Christian into a serious Holy Spirit led, Christ following man of God! To say I am proud of his spiritual progress would be a massive understatement.

Through the pages of *"Faith Hounds: A Relentless Pursuit"*, Will documents his personal quest for praying prayers that get real and tangible answers. I've always been impressed with his "never give up" attitude as he struggled to understand and activate genuine faith in his personal life. He's a young man who learns from both the Word of God and his own failures. What could God actually desire more from us than that?

I believe you will relate to Will's story and learn much from the discoveries he has made on his journey of a "relentless pursuit"! I'm also convinced that following Will's example of searching for truth will result in your own experience of the abundant life that Jesus came to give!

—Pastor David Brown
Of David Brown Ministries davidbrownministries.org
Former Senior Pastor of Victory Church in Amarillo Texas
Pastoral Staff of Abundant Church in El Paso Texas

A Message from the Author

ONE OF MY FAVORITE Scriptures is Jeremiah 33:3, *"Call to me and I will answer you, and will tell you great and hidden things that you have not known."* I surely hope you don't think that Scripture means I am claiming to be some all-knowing person who is boasting about his own wisdom and promising to lead you, the reader, into a utopia of wisdom and truth. That's not the case at all. The Lord whispered that Scripture to my heart when I began my journey in Him, while pursuing answers to my prayers. Like John the Baptist, I am only pointing the way to the One whose Holy Name I am not fit to even utter. The message I am sharing in this book is only to highlight His truth and His glory because all that I have is a gift from the Master's hands.

This book is a culmination of a seven-year period of time when God showed me things that I could not have even imagined, like Jeremiah 33:3 said, *". . . great and mighty things that I did not know."* As I went further down this road of revelation, I found that it was an answered prayer. When I was a young boy, I would sit and talk to God for what seemed like hours in my room at night looking through the window at a West Texas starry sky. I would talk to Him about all sorts of topics, but I distinctly remember I had one dominating request. I would always ask, *"Lord, make me your microphone, use me to get your message out there in the world."* He has answered my childhood prayer. I am not a singer like my wife, or a pastor like countless family members, but this book and the written word is my microphone, and I am thankful to use this platform to proclaim the goodness of God and His love for us, which gives us the ability to have a remarkable life through Him.

"This book will change the world because it will change someone's world."

—WILL MITCHELL

Acknowledgments

THERE ARE SO MANY PEOPLE that had a hand in the creation of this book. First, I thank the Lord who blessed me with this knowledge and deeper understanding of Him. Second, I thank my wife Amber, my mother who has been a great supporter and my late father who passed away before this book was published. Also I thank my editor Jeanne, my pastors and the man who I consider my spiritual Father who taught me to read and study the Word, David Brown. Consequently, I would be remiss if I did not thank the most important group of people, you the readers. You have spent your most valuable asset to read this book. I'm not talking about money, although that is a useful asset, and I greatly appreciate your purchase. However, I mean your most important commodity, your time. We all want more time and can never get it back. I am honored that you are spending your precious time reading this book.

Jesus Is the Cake

PICKING UP THIS BOOK and reading the title, many people likely think this book primarily talks about chasing God or seeking a godly life with the Lord. These thoughts are not wrong; however, before we discuss our pursuit of God, let's talk about how he first pursued us.

Lamentations 3:22 is a very popular Scripture usually used to show how God's forgiveness towards us is new every day. Let me share another thought this Scripture alludes to using the King James Version, *"It is of the Lord's mercies that we are not consumed, because his compassions fail not. They are new every morning."* When looking at the word "mercies" here, the Hebrew word *ḥesed*[1] is used and can mean "zeal." One definition of zeal states "with great energy or enthusiasm in pursuit of a cause or an objective."[2] Reading this Scripture with these definitions, the Scripture says: *"It is of the Lord's zeal [His great energy and enthusiasm] that we are not consumed, because his compassions fail not. They are new every morning."* Now take a step back and ask, "What cause and objective does God energetically and enthusiastically pursue every morning?" Friends, the "objective" is all of us, and the cause is having and maintaining an intimate relationship with us. Let me show how he continues to have zeal for us every day.

Jesus said in John 10:10 that he *"has come to give us life and life more abundantly."* Most people flock to this Scripture when

1. H2617 Ḥesed Strong's Hebrew
2. *Zeal* English Definition Meaning

they are believing God for an answer to prayer and only focus on the tail end of the Scripture. However, before we get to the *"have it more abundantly"* part, we have to understand what Jesus meant by first saying *"I have come to give you life."* Jesus is this life. I believe that in the first part of this Scripture, he explains how he came to give us an eternal life with him and God the Father. The second part of the Scripture, *"and have it more abundantly,"* means the physical life, while we are here on earth, our day in and day out. But before we dive into and pursue the individual promises of God, the *"have it more abundantly"* (i.e., health, prosperity and so on), it is vital, absolutely fundamental that we understand the God of the promise. Too many times in my own life, I got caught up in these individual promises, which is fine in its own right, but only pursuing the promises cannot and will not substitute for accepting Christ.

"Jesus is the Cake" means Jesus is the foundation. Seeking the individual promises of God such as provision, healing, peace, and joy is perfectly acceptable because that agrees with the Bible, but come on, when a person really grasps the love of God toward us, all these other promises are secondary . . . just "icing" on the cake. The Bible says in Ephesians that God chose a long time ago to adopt us into His family out of His good will. By using the word "chose," the writer is obviously telling us God had options, and he opted to choose us!

All the promises of God are the icing on the cake of Jesus. There are not too many people who eat only straight icing; they eat it on top of the cake. Without cake, icing is irrelevant because it has no foundation, so it has no place or purpose. So it is with God and His promises. Without having him in our lives first and a real relationship based on the Word of God, and on the Blood of Jesus Christ, then there is no sense in pursuing His promises because they are only for His children, according to Proverbs 15:29. I know this seems like a harsh statement, but it is Scripture. Now this begs the question *"How do we get this relationship and access to the Father with His promises?"* The answer is clearly laid out in Scripture and discussed later in this chapter.

JESUS IS THE CAKE

For now, I want to share a major revelation God gave me about who his son is really. While going through a season of learning from the Holy Spirit, I was employed at a juvenile detention center. My shift was 6:00 p.m. until 6:00 a.m. three days a week. After the kids were secured in their rooms from 10:00 p.m. until shift change at 6:00 a.m., I had nothing but time. My supervisor at the time gave me a book titled *The Fisherman* by Larry Huntsperger. The book is a fictional story of Paul's point of view when he met, walked, and lived with Jesus.[3] It is a great read. I find it funny how God can use anything to reach us. He used a donkey once to reach Balaam and a whale for Jonah. In this particular case, he used this book to make me realize that I knew the Lord as my Savior, but I didn't really understand him. Sad for me to admit that up to this point in my life, I had been walking with the Lord for about twelve years, and all that time I didn't really understand who he was and why what he did was so significant. My heart had been pricked, and I craved a deeper understanding of Who God and Jesus are.

One of the most familiar arguments against the Christian faith is, "*How can Jesus be God and man?*" For years I believed the Bible at face value when it states that Jesus is both God and man. I had always thought that God somehow turned himself into a baby and was born of Mary. This led to many other questions like, "*Well if God was here in human form, who was in heaven,*" and "*if God and Jesus are the same person, who in the world was Jesus talking to when he would pray to the Father. Would he then be praying to himself?*" Or my personal favorite, "*If God is Jesus and Jesus is God, then when Jesus was baptized in the river Jordan and a voice came out of heaven and said, "This is my* son *in him I am well pleased," then was God saying he was pleased with himself!?*" On a side note, isn't it ironic to see where our thinking and faith was compared to where it is now after we spend time with God and His Word? How great is our Father that he does not scold us for asking questions or get upset when we query about His Word! But like the loving Father he is, he takes time with us and shows us about what makes

---

3. Huntsperger, *Fishermen: Novel*, 1–253

us curious. The Bible says in James 1:5 that if we lack wisdom come to him because he loves to help!

Who He Is:

Simply put . . . Jesus is the physical form of an unseen God, so Jesus was and is God in the flesh. The Bible says in Colossians that Jesus is the firstborn over all creation, and out of him all things were created. To the critics of our faith, this area is a platform they would likely use to try to "disprove" our faith. In journalism and debate, this argument is called the *"got ya"* question. They may say, "Explain how Jesus is God" and then demand proof. However, I have learned in walking with the Lord for roughly fifteen years that there are many truths and claims the Bible makes that are beyond human comprehension. God is so immense that we cannot fully wrap our feeble human minds around him. I do believe that God understands this about His creation, so he reveals himself to us through His various Names throughout the Bible. One of these Names is simply I AM. In John chapter eight, Jesus described himself as "I AM," and our job, as Bible believing Christians, is to take those words at face value and believe that Jesus is God because he said he is. We must understand that if God (who is absolute Truth) claims to be something then we must believe those claims by faith as Truth. Any declaration that Jesus is God is one of these claims to trust. Along with the Bible, many great books and research tools are available to help people dig deeper into this topic, however in respect for the Lord and out of reverent fear that I might somehow misspeak about Jesus, I will just leave it at that. Jesus is God, end of story. An old song that is one of my favorites says in the chorus, "I believe You are who You say You are, and that will never change." I am thoroughly convinced that this has to be the attitude of every Bible believing Christian. Jesus is who he says he is, and that will never change.

Jesus Is the Cake

What He Did:

The Bible says that Jesus lowered himself to come into humanity, and then further humbled himself by obeying God unto death being the sacrificial lamb that all humanity needed to get back to the Father. To me, the fact the Bible used the phrase "He obeyed the Father" even holds more weight because it points to the fact the Jesus had a choice, and he did not have to die for us, but he did. Now keep in mind that we were created for His pleasure and were always supposed to be in a close relationship with him, but sin separated us from God. So, God loved us so much and wanted us back that he decided that he had to find a way to buy us back.

The only way to do this was through a worthy sacrifice, and since blood is the requirement to atone for sin (Lev 17:11; Heb 9:22), the only worthy blood was that of God. God saw the only blood that would meet His criteria belonged to him and him son, Jesus. So, Jesus was the only One who did what had to be done, because he was the only one who was able to do it. However, there was a problem, God's blood could not be spilled in His divine state; no one could kill him. Jesus obeyed the Father, lowered himself and voluntarily put aside his divinity to become a man who could shed the blood that was needed and ultimately die a sinner's death, even though he was innocent. His obedience makes it possible that through faith in him, we can be brought back to God our Father, our Creator (Phil 2:6–11).

Also, the Lord could not be tempted in Their divinity (James 1:13). But the Bible says that in lowering himself to become a man, it made him vulnerable to be tempted. In order for him to get the victory over sin, he had to face it on our human level since he could not sin on His God level. Since he did overcome sin, His sacrifice was worthy (2 Cor 5:21). Think of it like this . . . one cannot get victory over something if one never faces it. Obviously, I was not there, and the Bible simply says, *"He so loved the world,"* but I like to think that the Lord said, *"I want my creation back!"* The Father and the son looked around heaven and saw there was no blood strong enough to buy us back except the blood of God

(Acts 20:28), so Jesus said, *"I'll do it. I will go and win our loved ones back, Father!"*

Why It Is Important:

Now people may be asking, *"In a book about faith and answered prayer, why is this so important?"* Like most concepts in life, we must have a grasp on the fundamentals before we can move on to the advanced. The foundation of Christianity and an eternal relationship with God is understanding and believing by faith that Jesus did what he did. The Bible says that he was given a Name above all names and highly exalted. Imagine that you are in the back of a long line to enter an exclusive place or event. Someone you know and have a relationship with passes by everyone and goes ahead to the front door. This person then looks back and calls your name, motioning for you to come to the front, too. That is what Jesus did for us. When he received the highest status based on His sacrifice and obedience to the Father, he then turned around and gave that status to all who believe and follow him. First and foremost, knowing this and believing what the Bible says about Jesus is paramount for salvation and to spend eternity with God. The Bible plainly states in John 3:16 *"whoever believes in him will have eternal life."* No matter what we are pursuing in this world or what we want, it cannot compare to living in eternity with God. It is not just believing that there was a man named Jesus, who lived and died, but also acknowledging that he is the Messiah, the only way to the Father, believing the fact that His blood is the only thing that can wash away the sins of mankind and following him all the days of our lives. Also, since Jesus faced sin and won, he was given all authority and power in heaven and earth (Matt 28:18). But he didn't stop there, he gives this power and authority to us when we use His name and operate in His will (Luke 10:19, Mark 16:17–20).

Remember the Bible tells us multiple times that the individual promises of God are for His children only. However, once a person becomes His child through believing in Jesus and His sacrifice, I think it is easy to focus on the gifts and forget the Giver.

I believe a person shouldn't want a knowledge of Who God is just to get things from him. *Think about it, would you want someone to be your friend or only come around you when they want something?* I made this mistake myself in my walk with the Lord. I found myself only coming around to talk to him when I needed something, treating him like a fast-food joint, instead of a loving Father who gave everything he had just to bring me back to him. I told myself recently that I go to Burger King only when I want a burger; I refuse to treat Jesus like this, only coming to him when I want something like I'm a spoiled, entitled kid. I encourage everyone, before reading any further, to make sure to understand and follow this first and most important step. Become a child of the King by believing in Jesus that he is the Only way to the Father. Believe in His death, burial and resurrection. Then walk in close relationship with him, repenting from sin and following him. It's a weak attempt but this is how I sum up all that Father God and his son Jesus did for us. Remember at any given time in human history, he could have looked at what we were and what we would become; and he could have chosen to look at all the pain and suffering we would inflict on each other; not to mention the times we would spit in His face and completely disregard him; and he could have decided that we are not worth His sacrifice. But he didn't. Out of pure love and desire, he decided to complete His plan to save us with His own blood. All with the goal to have His loved ones back and to be in close relationship with us.

> *You must worship no other gods, for the Lord, whose very name is Jealous, is a God who is passionate about His relationship with you.* (Exodus 34:14)

Follow Your New Leader:

After people are "in" God via being in the body of Christ by becoming Christians, it is absolutely vital that we follow him in everything we do. When I first really grabbed hold of this idea, it changed the way I thought completely because it taught me two concepts. The first and most important step of following is we must allow someone to lead. This concept possesses a major problem for some because in order to be led by someone we have to give that person permission to lead. Secondly, the other scary thing about following the Lord is the guarantee that I will get cut. Jesus calls it "pruning" in the Gospel of John, but it's the same thing as cutting. No one likes to be cut; it hurts. Jesus is not talking about a physical cutting that draws blood, but a spiritual cutting that draws obedience. The Lord showed me that *pruning is a process* because, if a plant is pruned all at once, it will dry out and die. Some folks may think that when they become Christians and begin to follow the Lord that all their past issues will just disappear. But as all sheep of the Most High will tell, "that ain't happenin' captain." The man who was an alcoholic may still struggle, and the woman with lust in her heart will still face it daily. But thanks to our gracious and perfect Savior, he prunes us, day–by–day . . . week–by–week . . . month-by-month. he cuts away the old and replaces it with His new, and the reason he does this is simple. Jesus didn't do all he did just for us to have a hope and a future in eternity only. No, he gives us a hope and future in this life, as well (Jeremiah 29:11). Remember Jesus nailed the point home in John 10:10 when he said that he came to give us an abundant life. Over the years many people have watered down this word "abundant" to just mean money and possessions, but it means so much more. The original context of the word means: superior, extraordinary, surpassing, uncommon, superiority, remarkable. But in order to live the kind of life he intended for us to have, we must follow him and allow him to do what shepherds do, he leads.

Personally, I struggled with this issue because over the years I had developed a fear that Jesus would not lead me like he promised. This climaxed to the belief that I imagined I was actually bugging God when I would ask for wisdom over an issue and what he wanted me to do. However, I finally came to the realization that if I was actively pursuing God for wisdom, but doubted I was hearing from him, then I was basically calling him a liar and claiming he wasn't keeping His end of all His promises that talk about

His leadership if we pursue him. This stronghold I developed was finally broken down when the Holy Spirit showed me through Scripture and spoke to my heart one day saying, *"If I blessed Solomon for only asking for wisdom, what makes you think I would be mad at you for asking for it?"* This is true because in 1 Kings, God was ready to give Solomon anything he wanted, but all the man asked for was wisdom to lead God's people and do God's will. As a result, God was so impressed by this request he not only gave Solomon wisdom, but also gave him the money, wealth, notoriety, and material things asked for by any average person. Remember, Solomon pursued God's Kingdom first, and as a result, he was given everything else. Keep that point in mind, because we will explore that later in the book. To push this point deeper, the Lord led me to see, *"If he put such esteem and importance on wisdom. Why would he not give it plainly when I ask him for it?"* Again, this was proven true by the Bible in paraphrased Proverbs, "In all you're getting, get understanding." Here is another way to look at this; the Bible is filled with what I call "super Scripture sightings." When a Scripture in one Bible book fits perfectly like a puzzle piece with another Scripture from an entirely different Bible book. When these verses are read together, it gives a shot of adrenaline to our faith. In the area of guidance and following the Lord, look at Psalm 32:8 and Jeremiah 10:23. In Psalms 32:8 God says, *"I will instruct you and teach you in the way you should go; I will counsel you with my loving eye on you."* While Jeremiah 10:23 says, *"Lord, I know that people's lives are not their own; it is not for them to direct their steps."* So, the "super Scripture sighting" would read:

"God will instruct you and teach you the way you should go, and with a loving eye counsel you (Psalm 32:8)., *because* your life is not your own and it's not for man to direct his own steps (Jeremiah 10:23.)"

I will continue to share these "super Scripture sightings" in various areas throughout the rest of the book, and also know that I am not taking away or adding anything to God's Holy Word. He doesn't need Will Mitchell to make His Word better, which is perfect as is. I am simply showing the revelation I have received while reading these verses. So anytime there is an italicized *because*, that is just me combining scriptures.

The enemy knows how important it is that we are led by God and stay in relationship with him. Having an open line of communication is vital in every aspect of life and even more so spiritually. This is why the first spiritual "attack" ever recorded on the human race was when the Devil went to Eve in Genesis 3:1 and asked her, *"Has God really said . . . ?"* regarding the command God gave about not eating from the Tree Of The Knowledge Of Good And Evil. It seems the enemy's strategy is, *"If I can get them to doubt that they hear from God, then I will not even have to go after the promises of God in their lives."* If the seed and weed of doubt toward God and His promise of His willingness to lead us is allowed to sprout in our heart, doubt will kill the flower of faith before it has a chance to grow. To the one who doubts, the Bible makes it clear in James, *"That man should not expect to receive anything from the Lord."*

Another great lesson the Lord taught me was how simplistic it is to hear from God. Over the years, our culture has made hearing from God seem either spooky or ridiculous, but Jesus said in John 14:21, *"He who has my commandments and keeps them, it is he who loves me. And he who loves me will be loved by my Father, and I will love him and manifest Myself to him."* That word *manifest* in the text can also be translated *plainly show,* so the Bible is promising us here that Jesus will plainly show himself. When something is plain, it's simple.

To strengthen this point, the Bible said in Matthew 18:3 that unless we are like children, then we cannot enter the Kingdom. To most kids, everything is simple, and nothing is complicated. Also remember that when a response comes, it always has peace attached to it, if it's from Jesus. God is not the author of confusion, so then why would he make hearing, learning and receiving from him confusing? In Hosea 4:6, *"My people are destroyed because of lack of knowledge,"* so it seems God puts a premium on gaining knowledge and understanding, if the very lack of it would destroy us. I had always felt that I was making things too complicated, however I have to remember that when I was a boy and asked my dad a question, he answered immediately and without anger. *So why would God be any different?!* Here are some quick tips from what I learned about hearing from God:

- What comes from God will bring peace (John 14:27*).* Sometimes the answer is not obviously in the Bible, but if it's truly from the Lord, it will have His fruit of peace.
- If what you feel is from the Holy Spirit, ask yourself, *"Would that be something the enemy would say?"* For example, say you want wisdom about how to deal with someone at work. You feel led to pray for this person with them. You can be confident that this nudge in your heart is not from the enemy because he would not encourage you to pray for anyone.
- What is said may go against the knowledge of the world. For example, the world may say that a person has no future because of what they look like or where they are from. But God says otherwise.
- What is said will always line up with God's Word. Remember, if you ask for anything that agrees with His will, there are a multitude of promises in His Word that he will use to answer you. Godly wisdom definitely agrees with His will. So we can be 100% sure he will give it, when we ask.

From the Spirit, through the Soul and to the Body

IN ORDER TO BE a faith hound and relentlessly go after all God's promises, it's not only important to know *who* the promise comes from, but also *where* the promise is. One of the most significant revelations I have ever received while in my walk with the Lord was understanding how God speaks and how His promises come to pass in the physical flesh realm. My mistake had been that I was expecting some supreme vision or angelic visitation for me to receive God's promises. I fell into thinking, *"Lord, show me a sign,"* but quickly learned that this kind of request could be dangerous. Yes, God most certainly does give dreams, visions and voices to our physical bodies; however more often than not, His response is in the still quiet whisper, like it was for Elijah. Also, I learned that the "show me a sign" thinking could be obliged, not by God, but by the enemy. If it is really the Lord, the "message" revealed will always be in agreement with the Bible, because His Word is the reflective surface of His will.

Before we search deeper into this understanding, let's review to get an understanding of human beings. Humans are not just flesh, bone and blood, but three-part beings. A person is a *spirit* who has a *soul* and lives in a *body*.

From the Spirit, through the Soul and to the Body

The Three Parts of Humans:

Body	+	Soul	+	Spirit
(Physical)		(Also known as the heart, mind emotions)		(Connection piece to God)

We may wonder again, *"Why is this important?"* It's crucial to understand not only *Who* God is, but also *What* God is. John 4:24 says plainly that God is a Spirit, and since he is a Spirit, then His promises that we believe must be spirit, also. Since we cannot see in the spiritual realm and cannot comprehend the things of God through our physical bodies, we need some help. The Bible is that help as it is the *mirror* that shows the things of the spirit and reveals spiritual truth.

Keep in mind that the spirit realm is more real than the physical because the Bible says in Hebrews that what we see was made from what we can't see. The coffee we may be drinking while reading this book was in the spirit before it ever ended up in our hands. It's there now because someone pulled it out of the spirit realm with the idea of brewing coffee and making it a drink.

In James 1:24, the Bible talks about the Word being a mirror and likens it to someone who looks into a physical mirror but does nothing about what he sees. Our physical eyes have never seen our faces without the help of a reflective surface. The reflective surface shows the *truth* of the appearance of our faces. Same thing with the Bible, . . . our body nor soul (mind, heart) has ever "seen" the spiritual dimension, or the actual truth of what God has said. The *only* way to actually see the truth about these things is through the reflective surface of the Bible which reflects or *shows* the holy perfect things of the Lord.

To understand this point further, in John 6:63, Jesus says that His words are *spirit* and are *truth*. A powerful way for us to look at this concept is to say that *"every time I read His Word, God's will is (insert scriptural promise) towards me, because if it is in the Bible, then the words I am reading are the reflective surface showing me what God wants."*

Personally, I had the flow of God's response wrong. I thought messages came from God straight to the flesh, but the Lord showed me that he has already spoken in His Word, which is the Bible. Then when a person gets right with God through faith in Jesus, they are given a new spirit, God's spirit, the Holy Spirit.

A deeper look at the three parts of a *saved* person is:

Body (Flesh): Is not saved or made perfect because if you were fat before you got saved, you will be fat afterwards.

Soul (Mind/Emotions): Is not saved because if you knew a dirty joke or pornography website before you got saved, you would still know it afterwards.

Spirit: Your spirit is saved and made new to be like Jesus when you believe and follow him. In Romans, the Bible states, *"You, however, are not in the realm of the flesh but are in the realm of the Spirit, if indeed the Spirit of God lives in you."* Second Corinthians makes this truth more relevant by saying, *"Therefore, if anyone is in Christ, the new creation has come: The old has gone, the new is here!"*

The flow of receiving the manifestations of God into a saved person's life is:

From the spirit because . . .

Now that a believer has a new spirit, it is the connection piece to God through Jesus. It is what God has saved, and where God communicates to us, because that's where he is.

Through the soul because . . .

Where your mind aka your heart is, where belief in His Word happens, according to Romans 10:10, and where the issues of life come from Proverbs 4:23.

From the Spirit, through the Soul and to the Body

Then lastly to the body . . .

Since our spirit is new and right with God, His promises can finally manifest in our physical world. Also, flesh is what is necessary for God to operate in this realm.

I kept falling into another mental trap by thinking I had the promise, when it actually manifested in my life. However, this is in contrast to what the Word says. In this world of "see to believe," we forget this is not how God operates. In 2 Peter 1:3 the Bible says, *"God has made all things available that pertain to life and godliness."* Now the question a maturing Christian must ask is, *"Does the promise I'm believing in God to fulfill pertain (agree with) to a godly life?"* If so, then the promise has already been completed and is waiting in the spirit realm.

In Mark 11:24, Jesus told us *"When you pray, believe you that have received it and it shall come to pass."* Received is the past tense, as in *already done*. Shall is the future and represents *physical manifestation* that comes later. This is why it is vital our actions show that we believe that we already have God's promise in our spirit by the works from our physical being. We do this to confirm that it's not an expectation based on believing it *"will"* show. Rather, it's an expectation based on *"we already have it."* Remember that our actions show what's in our spirit. When I finally understood this belief down in my heart, it bonded me deeper to the Lord because I could see more of the benefits that Jesus paid for that came with my salvation. Jesus is the key and lynch pin to connecting us back to the Father. Not only for salvation, but for a life filled with blessing and prosperity. I'm not talking about just money either, but the true definition of prosperity, which is *whole and healthy in all areas, lacking nothing.*

When I wonder about Jesus being crucified, I get the image in my heart that while he hung there, beaten beyond human recognition, exhausted, bleeding and having all the weight of humanity's sin on him, he looked up and mustered the strength to say, as the Bible tells in John 19:30, *"It is finished."* He did not just mean His human life and our salvation, but also the process to give us access to all of God's promises was finished. This is why the Bible records that the veil in the temple, the physical material separating humanity from God, was ripped through the middle when Jesus died. Now all those who believe in him have access to Almighty God, our Father.

Prayer

WHILE WORKING ON THIS book, the Holy Spirit put such a burden on my heart to learn more about prayer. I felt that if I dug deeper into the subject, a revelation was waiting for me, a revelation on par to that when God gave me the subject matter for this book, and boy, was I right.

In the world of marketing there is a concept called "market saturation." This is when there is so much of a certain product that the company who created it will not experience any more growth. I believe this concept is true in different areas of life also, especially in the area of prayer. Now hear me out before closing this book and throwing it away. I am not saying prayer has lost its power, and I am definitely not saying that the Lord, who invites us to pray, will stop us from growing in His influence or power over us. However, I am saying that I think the true concept of prayer has been lost by some. Too many times I have heard prayer talked about as a last-ditch effort to get something done or portrayed as a ritualistic mundane practice that a person dreads like they dread going to the dentist. Maybe some feel that prayer is boring and "doesn't work." These attitudes simply should not be the case, when thinking about prayer. In the short time I have been studying more about prayer, I have found that prayer is both relational and powerful.

In all subjects I study, I like to establish some simple base of questions. One of those questions I always ask is "*What is _____?*" The blank there is filled with whatever topic I am studying, so in this case, it would be "*What is prayer*?" Simply put, prayer is talking to the Lord; however, I also came to the realization that the Bible talks about prayer in many ways. Asking, beseeching, supplication... These are all words used to talk about prayer. The Bible puts prayer at such a paramount, that some form of it is mentioned over 375 times throughout its pages. This naturally leads me to the other question I ask when studying, "*Why?*" Why does God want us to pray; what does it do? Like a kid opening up his birthday gift, I was so excited to dig into this topic and see what knowledge the Lord had for me, and once again he did not disappoint. Maybe you are asking yourself, "*Why do I need to pray?*" Let me answer this question with another question, "Why do you need to eat?" Because it's necessary, right? That is the same reason we must pray; it is a necessity to all areas of life.

Relationship:

Prayer is first and foremost spending time with God. Everyone knows I love the outdoors. Primarily I love to fish, but also, I just like to see nature and how God designed it. I will catch myself at times watching documentaries about faraway places that I will likely never see in person. When I look at these places, I always come back to one common thought that the God of the universe, the One who created all these places and much more, thought enough of me to invite me to talk to him. Even more so, he wants to talk back! In Exodus, God tells us to worship no one else but him because he is passionate about His relationship with us. When we are passionate about something, we want to spend time with it. God is passionate about us and wants to hear from us. Another example from the book of Genesis says that God came down in the cool of the day looking for Adam and Eve to talk to them. Now people have argued for years whether "cool of the day" was morning or evening, but I don't think that's important at all. The part of this story that makes me pick my jaw off the floor in awe is that God came down to spend time and talk with His creation. If we really think about it, the only two recorded times that God came down to earth was to spend time with His creation and then to save His creation.

The relational aspect of prayer is examined in Ephesians 3:12. The Living Bible translation says, *"Now we can come fearlessly right into God's presence, assured of his glad welcome when we come with Christ and trust in him."* Thankfully my parents and I have a very loving relationship. As a matter of fact, it is because of them I have the relationship I have with the Lord, because I saw their passion, love and pursuit of Jesus, while I was growing up. Most parents have nicknames for their kids. My dad, who recently passed away, would call me "Tank," and my mama calls me "Man," which is shortened from "Munchie Man," which she called me when I was a boy. As long as I can remember, no matter their moods or circumstances, I can always count on hearing them say, "Hey Tank" or "Hey Man" and feel their glad welcome whenever I would speak to them. If we are believers in Christ Jesus, according to Ephesians 3:12, we can come boldly in the throne of God and expect the Most High's glad welcome. Imagine with me going right up to the throne of God in prayer, and God standing with arms wide open and saying, *"Hey son, daughter,"* or in my case, "Hello *Tank*," while wrapping His arms around us and telling us to take a seat, so we can talk! Always remember that we are encouraged to come talk to the Father. First Peter 5:7 AMP says, *"casting all your cares [all your anxieties, all your worries, and all your concerns, once and for all] on him, for he cares about you [with deepest affection, and watches over you very carefully]."* When we are in a relationship with someone, we care about them deeply. This verse promises us that God watches over us very carefully and wants us to give him all our wants, issues, and problems in prayer.

I will never forget when the Lord opened my eyes and showed me just how much he cares for us. Outside of the Cross, there are a multitude of examples, but the one that really hit home to me is how much he actually wants to spend time with us. John 4:23 in the King James Version states, *"But the hour cometh, and now is, when the true worshippers shall worship the Father in spirit and in truth: for the Father seeketh such to worship him."* The word *seeketh* in the Greek can also mean to *crave,* so it's sound to believe that God craves us to worship him in spirit and truth. *But why does the Maker of heaven and earth crave my small, insignificant, raggedy worship?* I finally came to realize that it's not for His vanity, God is God, and beside him there is no other. He doesn't need anything from us. Nothing, but Scripture tells us why he craves and looks for our worship in Psalm 22:3, *"But thou art holy, O thou that inhabitest the praises of Israel." Inhabitest* is an old English word that also means to *sit down in.*[1] I am convinced that the Lord craves our worship (John 4:23) because he wants to sit down with us (Psalm 22:3). Therefore friends, before we move on to discuss the other benefits of prayer, take a minute to realize that the Most High wants, he craves, His creation. This is why he knelt in the mud to create us and why he sent his son to pay for us. All to bring us back into a relationship with him.

Intervention:

Prayer is asking the Lord to intercede on the behalf of ourselves and others. When we look at Scriptures that deal with prayer like Matthew 8:13 and 2 Chronicles 7:14, they specifically use the phrases, " . . . *it will be done for you*" or "*I will . . .* " These phrases hold promises that God will do for us, on our behalf. If prayer is the act of asking God to intercede on our behalf, then His individual promises are guarantees of that intervention. For example, suppose a man in Bangladesh is praying the prayer of repentance right now and asking God to forgive his sin, and wash him in the blood of Christ. This person is asking for God's intervention in his physical and eternal life. Therefore, Scripture like John 3:16 is the promise of God's intervention for this man. Meanwhile, imagine a Christian woman in Alaska asking the Lord for financial increase so she can do more for others and give more. Then Scriptures like 2 Corinthians 9:6–9 would cover her with God's promise of intervention. The intervention of God means that when we pray, we are

---

1. Martinez, *"God Inhabits,"* para. 3.

talking to the only One who has the authority and capability to keep His promises to us.

The Dispenser of Good:

Prayer is going to the One who has all the goods! James 1:17 (KJV) says, *"Every good gift and every perfect gift is from above, and comes down from the Father of lights, with whom there is no variation or shadow of turning."* This verse always amazes me how something so simple can be so powerful and so overlooked. I am convinced that under this umbrella of James 1:17 rests all the individual promises of God like provision, healing, forgiveness and basically anything good for us. God is a distributor of good gifts; and there are multiple promises in the Bible to back this claim, and I have many personal examples, as well.

For years I thought that God only cared about the major issues in my life like my salvation or health. I never thought he cared about the little daily life happenings that might mean the world to me. But in true loving Father fashion, the Holy Spirit showed me that this couldn't be further from the truth, and for proof we need only to look at Jesus' first miracle.

In the book of John, the Bible tells Jesus' first recorded miracle. In the story of the "Wedding at Cana," during the wedding celebration, the hosts ran out of wine. Mary, Jesus' mother, came to him for help because she knew he could solve the problem. Jesus then told her that this was not the issue for His time to start His ministry, but he performed the miracle anyway, by turning the water into wine that was better than the original wine. Not taking liberties with Scripture, but I think what happened is Jesus performed this miracle because it was the perfect time to bring Glory to the Father, and he was not going to pass on that opportunity.

When looking at this miracle again, it proves the Lord cares about every aspect of our lives. I have researched those days, and it would have been a great disgrace for the groom and his family who were hosting the party to run out of wine. Furthermore, wine is nowhere near to being a necessity, because it doesn't have anything to do with our health, let alone our salvation. Also, they were at a party, not at synagogue or some other holy place. Yet Jesus provided the wine anyway... *but why?* I believe this story ties back to John 10:10, and the *"have it more abundantly"* portion of that promise. Jesus is all for us having a good time, as long as it doesn't lead to sin and its consequences. Therefore, we can safely conclude that God is a God who cares about our joy, as well as our souls.

After walking with the Lord all this time, I have seen this play out in my life and learned that he is the God Who cares about the important (big) things, but he also cares about the insignificant (small) things in life. I will never forget when I was a junior in college with no money at all, like most kids. It was my dad's birthday, and I wanted to get him a gift. I prayed simply, "Lord bless me to somehow come up with some money to get him a good gift." That night after class and basketball practice, I went to a young adults' event at church and was picked to participate in a silly little ice breaker trivia game to start the night off. It was all in good fun, but the winner got a $50 Visa gift card. I made it to the final round, and guess what, I won the whole thing! I gave the gift card to my dad inside a birthday card and was able to bless him. Now reading this, there is no way for anyone to understand how much I knew this silly little event was all God, because I *never* win anything like this *ever*. I don't expect anyone to fathom this tiny miracle because it doesn't seem like much to the random person. But to me, much like the people at the wedding in Cana, this miracle meant the absolute world, and that night, I knew it was the Lord showing me that when he instructed us to cast our cares on him it's because he cares about every aspect of our lives, even the small areas.

On the other side of this coin, we need to consider what is not happening in our lives. I will dive into this topic in a later chapter about hindrances, but for now, simply look at the logic in James 1:17. If all good things come from God, and I am not getting what I want in my life... *Am I even asking?* James 4:2–3 makes this clear and simple,

> *You want what you don't have, so you scheme and kill to get it. You are jealous of what others have, but you can't get*

> it, so you fight and wage war to take it away from them. Yet you don't have what you want because you don't ask God for it. And even when you ask, you don't get it because your motives are all wrong—you want only what will give you pleasure.

This entire Scripture is true, but for the sake of explaining this concept, I want to focus on the end of verse two, "... *Yet you don't have what you want because you don't ask God for it.*"

We may not be seeing answers to prayer in our lives simply because we don't ask, for whatever reason. It could be because we think our desires are too big, too small, not important or a myriad of other reasons. All those reasons and excuses are lies from hell itself. I encourage us all to get in the Word and in prayer; find out what God says about the desires of our hearts and simply ask.

Coming Close:

This area was the crown jewel of the revelation God gave me about prayer. James 4:8 in the Bible says, *"Draw near to God and he will draw near to you, cleanse your hands, you sinners; and purify your hearts, you double-minded."* The start of the Scripture tells us to draw near to God, which means come close to him. When we pray, we are doing just that, correct? That is simple enough, but "*Why draw near to God?*" Among the many reasons we need to pray, one stands out that the Lord kept showing me. When someone "*draws near*" to us, we have just entered their presence, which means they are close enough where their influence is all around us. James is telling us to draw near to God, not for him to be in our presence, let's be real, our presence is really nothing to boast about, and he is already omnipresent. However, what the verse is saying is come close to God because when we do, we know he draws near to us bringing His presence with him. We are in the very presence of God when we pray and come to the Father in Jesus' Name. So when I came to this conclusion, it naturally led me to my next question. *What is in God's presence?* This is what the Bible says about what comes with the presence of God:

- Freedom from bondage–2 Corinthians 3:17
- Healing–2 Chronicles 7:14
- Fullness of joy–Psalm 16:11
- Rest–Exodus 33:14
- Relationship–Genesis 3:8
- Protection–Psalm 91, Proverbs 18:10
- Comfort–Psalm 23:4
- Peace–Philippians 4:7

Jesus died for all these benefits that are just waiting for us in the presence of God. God's love is so strong towards his creation that he sent his son who went willingly to die and to be the sacrifice needed to allow us to come in God's presence with access to all these blessings. With all these benefits just waiting for us, one would think that we would sprint towards a place of prayer, where everyone in the whole world would set aside parts of the day to spend time in the presence of God, right? In theory, this prayer time should happen. However, we have an opposing and interfering issue, and his name is Satan.

If I were the enemy, and I did not want people to experience anything good at all and I just wanted life to be full of misery and pain, I would do all I could do to keep people from anyone who would help or benefit them. That's what Satan does. He absolutely hates humanity because we are made in God's image, and God went to great lengths to save us. No wonder, the enemy attacks us with distractions, fears, doubt and a plethora of other evil to keep us from a place of prayer. Satan knows that when we come close to God, God then comes close to us, and as a result, Almighty God's presence automatically gives us access to all those fantastic blessings that are just waiting for us.

Protection and Strength:

Prayer is also asking God to "have our backs" while asking him for strength. To say protection is a reason to pray may be the understatement of the year. We all need protection; we all need someone looking out for us, so why not the Almighty? The Lord blessed me with a major revelation on this subject because he helped me see that protection is an individual promise, like many of the benefits mentioned in the section about God being the dispenser of good, but it is much more. It is no coincidence that Jesus is called the "Lion and the Lamb." Obviously, he is the Lamb because he was our sacrifice for sin, and he is a Lion because he is mighty and the King. That fact is often lost on people that Jesus is a King in the sense of a protector and a conqueror. History tells us that every good king protected his kingdom and the people in it.

Proverbs 18:10 says, *"The name of the Lord is a strong tower; the righteous run to it and are safe."* It's worth noting that the word "safe" here means *inaccessibly high.* This promise makes us ask the questions, *"Safe from what? What is God making us safe from and inaccessible to?"* The answer is the enemy and all his attacks. The answer is safe from fear, inaccessible to the temptation of sin and all other wiles of the Devil. Remember from earlier in this chapter that when we pray, we draw near to God and as result, he draws near to us. Remember when he is near to us that brings His presence. This fact makes Proverbs 18:10 true because when we are in the tower of the Lord's Name and in His Holy Presence that evil attack of the enemy cannot be there to assault us, therefore making us "safe and inaccessible."

Another way to look at prayer is the strengthening effect it has on us, evident in Hebrews 4:16 when the Bible says, *"Let us therefore come boldly unto the throne of grace, that we may obtain mercy, and find grace to help in time of need."* Allow me to break this Scripture into meaningful parts. Obviously, the beginning of this passage is talking about prayer when it says to "... *come boldly to the throne of grace* ... " The word "grace" here is the Greek word *charis.* It appears twice, once describing God's throne and the second to depict an empowering. The latter part of the Scripture when *charis* appears means: *to strengthen, increase them in Christian faith or kindle them to exercise Christian virtues.* [2] Reading this Scripture with this understanding, it says, *"Let us therefore come boldly unto the throne of grace, that we may obtain mercy, and find the strengthening to exercise Christian virtues. Help in time of need."* Think of a time when believers need this strengthening to exercise their Christian virtues. I sure can. What about when we are tempted with sin, when our hearts are completely the Lord's, but we have sinful cravings so strong it makes our mouths water? Some people reading this may say they have not ever had any temptations like this, but I can attest and will admit I do. Whether folks admit it or not, we all have those "easily besetting sins" as the Bible calls them. It may be lust, it may be rage and it may be unforgiveness or hate. It doesn't really matter the specific sin, because we all have them. Just because we are followers of Christ now, do not think that the sin that once held us captive will just let us go without a fight. In fact, the Lord helped me to understand that *"the sin that once bound you will relentlessly pursue you until it gets you back into submission."* This is why the Bible tells us to be vigilant, because the enemy is looking for someone to devour, looking for a free slave to take back into the slavery of sin. This is why God's protection and strength are so key.

When we come to His throne, he promises us that we will receive *charis*, this strengthening to exercise our Christian virtue and resist the enemy. Second Corinthians 12:9 is a great verse to see how God culminates the importance of prayer when it comes to protection and strength. On the surface it is straightforward, *"And he said unto me, my grace is sufficient for thee: for my strength is made perfect in weakness. Most gladly therefore will I rather glory in my infirmities, that the power of Christ may rest upon me."* For years that Scripture has baffled me because I didn't understand how God's strength is made perfect when I am weak. God does not want us to come to him just for safety, as he said in Proverbs 18:10, but also to come for His grace and strength to do what we

---

2. *Charis* Meaning Bible-NT.

can't. In our everyday lives, we gravitate towards success and want to learn how someone accomplished what we could not. Take weight loss for example, maybe many of you have tried for years to lose fifty pounds. You have tried it your way forever but never succeeded, but then your friends who also needed to lose weight actually lost their sixty pounds and have kept it off. Naturally, you would go to them and get their secrets about how they lost their weight. Victory in this life is no different. When we come to the Lord in our weakness, His strength is made most effective because he is the only One who conquered sin and death and lives eternally in victory overall. We go to him to empower us to overcome every situation we may face because he is the only One who overcame every situation we will face.

The last piece of evidence I share advocating the protection of God when we pray and come to him is found in Philippians 4:6–7. This Scripture is quoted many times, and the New Living Translation version reads, *"Don't worry about anything; instead, pray about everything. Tell God what you need and thank him for all he has done. Then you will experience God's peace, which exceeds anything we can understand. His peace will guard your hearts and minds as you live in Christ Jesus."* This is a powerful promise of God because the Lord is encouraging us to pray, and then guarantees he will do His part and guard our hearts and minds. The word "guard" here is translated "keep" in the King James Version, which is *phroureō* in the Greek and means: *to guard, protect by a military guard, either to prevent hostile invasion, or to keep the inhabitants of a besieged city from flight*.[3] With this understanding, the Scripture could be read like this, *"Don't worry about anything; instead, pray about everything. Tell God what you need and thank* him *for all he has done. Then you will experience God's peace, which exceeds anything we can understand. His peace will guard [and protect your hearts and minds by military guard and prevent hostile invasion] as you live in Christ Jesus."* What could the hostile invasion be? It's the same as discussed earlier; it's all the attacks of the enemy. However, this promise comes with a stipulation, one that I never realized

---

3. *Phroureō* Meaning Bible-NT

until now. At the end of the verse, it says "... *as you live in Christ Jesus.*" The writer is saying that in order to get this military guard of our hearts and minds when we pray, we must be living in Christ. The meaning is actively following him. If we step outside of him in any way, then we have no right to expect this peace when we pray. It's no different from how the US military protects us because we are citizens of the country; in the same way, God will protect us because we are a part of His Kingdom.

I'll close this section with a dream the Lord gave me one night. I will be honest; it was right after I fell by doing my "easily besetting sin." I did not do the strategy I shared here: I did not pray, seek His protection or resist in any way. I just did what I wanted to do. After it was over, I felt the shame and guilt associated with sin. Then, I went to the Father through prayer, confessed it to him, asked for forgiveness and repented. That night I had a dream that was so real that I am sure I was in the very presence of God and His angels. When I woke up in the waking world, I wanted to go back to that place of the dream because I knew God was there. In the dream, I was in a cave, but it was not a dark and dank cave. A bunch of kids was there with me, and I was presenting an old school puppet show. The mood was light and fun, when suddenly something like cake frosting started falling down on us. There was so much frosting that it was piling up like a snowbank. Then all the kids and I started eating the sweet and tasty stuff. Once we had our fill, another adult appeared in the group and said, "Ok everyone, it's time to worship the Lord." The next part of this dream makes me convinced that this was a spiritual dream on a whole different level that I had never before experienced. A beautiful, out of this world melody was being sung by the kids and me. It sounded so heavenly; it was nothing like I have heard here in this world. The Bible talks about "heavenly worship," and I am convinced that was it. I cannot remember the whole song but just the chorus went like this:

> *What in the world do I say, when sin and the enemy call out my name? ... Je-sus! And tell me ... What in the*

world do I say to stop the attack and hold the wolves at bay? . . . Je-sus!

Over and over again throughout the next day that chorus played in my head. I know it was the Lord reminding me of this dream I shared. Always remember friends, when the wolves attack us, call our Lion, and when the enemy with his sin calls out our names, we call out to the King. Jesus!

The Hang Up:

Before I close this chapter, I would be remiss if I did not address what I believe is the number one reason we don't go to God in prayer and how the enemy weaponizes it. Fear is the reason we don't pray, and the Devil knows this and uses it to his advantage. Everything I shared in this chapter is just a fraction of the benefit of prayer. Satan knows this and will try his hardest to stop us from going to God in prayer. He knows the power of prayer and how it can render him inert in our lives. The Lord drew this parallel for me in my first book about divorce and the importance of communication between spouses. He showed me that in war, before the first bullet is shot or the first bomb is released, an invading nation simply cuts off the communication abilities of their enemy. By severing communication, the country being attacked cannot call for help or reach its allies. The same is true in our spiritual lives, Satan is the invader, and we are the invaded. If he can cut off our communication by using fear and other tactics, then he has us. One would think that since prayer is packed with such benefits, there would be a law that every Christian, world-wide, would spend at least an hour in God's presence praying. However, there isn't, and if some people are like me, sometimes we let the enemy's attack of fear be the primary culprit in stopping us. I was afraid to pray because I was afraid that God was mad at me and that I was too filthy to even think about talking to him. Like me, many may have told themselves, *"You claim to be this Jesus follower but look at what you did, and still do. Pathetic!"* Again, our sweet God, Who is slow to anger but rich in unfailing love, always reminds me that when we come to him through Jesus, he sees us clean and pure because of the blood of our Lamb. Look at the story of the "Prodigal Son." The book of Luke tells us that this guy blew off his father, spent his inheritance and fell to rock bottom. Once he got to his lowest point, he made the decision to go back home to his father, and at the very least, work as a servant. The Bible says something very interesting in Luke 15:20, *"But while he (the son) was still a long way off, his father saw him."* This indicates that the father was looking for his son, even when he knew his son was wrong. If that's not an intimate picture of God, then I don't know what is. In Genesis, God came looking for Adam when he already knew Adam sinned, yet God still looked saying, *"Adam where are you!?"* I encourage us all; do not be afraid to talk to the Almighty. Fear has no place when it comes to God other than the "fear" meaning respect for the Lord.

It finally dawned on me during my study of prayer and time with the Lord that I was thinking of prayer in a singular fashion, when it's multi-faceted. In the world of weightlifting, there are only two ways to train muscles: isolation vs. compound movement. Isolation is singular in nature; it means training one muscle at a time. Bicep curls are an example of this because they only focus on strengthening and building biceps. Compound movement, on the other hand, works several muscles at the same time. Burpees or pull-ups are fantastic examples of compound movement because those exercises work about five to ten muscles at the same time. All this time, I thought of prayer as an isolation, excessive activity doing only one thing at a time. After sitting at God's feet learning more, I now know prayer is a compound movement type of concept. When we pray, we are doing a burpee in the spirit world, working all the spiritual areas and much more!

Whatever the circumstance, I encourage us to draw near to God daily in prayer and stay in His presence. Set aside time, make it mandatory in our lives much like brushing our teeth. Maybe five minutes of time or fifty, stretched throughout the day or taken all at once. It really doesn't matter how we pray, as long as we do.

Remember that he is the dispenser of all good things, and more importantly, he just wants to talk to us, his kids, and spend time with us. Furthermore, when the fear of coming to God attacks us, combat it with the promise of Jesus when he said, *"All those the Father gives me will come to me and I will by no means cast them out."* When we do this, we will be experiencing His presence and will experience all that comes with it.

Another reason many people do not go consistently into prayer is because they simply feel like they do not have anything to say. As strange as that may seem, I understand this, and believe that those in this group fall into one of three categories. For one group, they may have a haughty mindset, thinking they have no reason to talk to God. The second group may feel like there are so many questions that they do not even know where to begin. The third group may feel like their prayers lack substance, so they feel it's a waste of time to the Lord. During the course of writing this book, I found myself in this last category. I felt that I was just rambling and not having any real quality time with the Master. Once again, the gentleness of the Holy Spirit led me to a revelation with this error in thinking. The Lord showed me that he is my Father by reminding me that I am a father, too. In doing so, I started thinking about my girls, and how they just come sit in the room with me while I'm in my office, or how they want to come sit in my boat when I am in the garage getting ready for a fishing trip. The Lord helped me remember how my heart feels when I ask them what they want, and all they say is, "Oh nothing Daddy, we just want to be with you." Mostly, I encourage us to never feel like we are wasting time with God, even if we just want to be around him, he loves us. Remember all the benefits that come by simply just being in His presence.

As for feeling our prayers lack substance, the Lord put me in remembrance of a sermon I heard when I was a boy. In the sermon my pastor broke down the Lord's Prayer into sections and showed how each part can be used to expand our own prayer lives. Most of us know the Lord's Prayer quoted in Matthew 6:9-13, when Jesus, the centerpiece of our faith, told us how to pray.

> *After this manner therefore pray ye: Our Father which art in heaven, Hallowed be thy name. Thy kingdom come, Thy will be done on earth, as it is in heaven. Give us this day our daily bread. And forgive us our debts, as we forgive our debtors and lead us not into temptation but deliver us from evil: For thine is the kingdom, and the power, and the glory forever, Amen.*

This is straightforward teaching; however, allow me to share the breakdown of each part of the prayer to see how much substance this simplistic prayer really holds:

Our Father who art in heaven, Hallowed be thy name

Here is the primary order of Jesus' prayer, and the first piece of bread in what I like to imagine as the "prayer sandwich." This part can also be considered worship. When we say this, we are establishing the order of God in our prayer and in our life. That he is King, and His name is hallowed or *hagiazō* in the Greek, which means "to declare holy."

Thy kingdom come, Thy will be done in earth, as it is in heaven:

This line further establishes our will for God's influence and desires to be done in our lives and on the Earth.

Give us this day our daily bread.

Finally, we get to the part of prayer that Jesus shows is time to ask for things in our own lives. Bread here is not just food, but it symbolizes provision for all our needs, desires and wants.

And forgive us our debts, as we forgive our debtors:

Obviously, this is when we ask the Lord to forgive our sins, sinful thoughts, issues, and weaknesses. This happens while we forgive those who have wronged us, whether the offense is known or unknown to us. Remember we need to forgive before we can be forgiven according to Matthew 6:15.

And lead us not into temptation but deliver us from evil:

Here we are asking the Lord to not allow us to be led into temptation, as we go throughout the day, while asking him to rescue us from evil in every form.

For thine is the kingdom, and the power, and the glory, forever, Amen:

This is the last piece of bread in the "prayer sandwich," and again this line establishes how the Lord is the Beginning and the End in our lives.

Please do not misunderstand; I am not saying that this is the exact layout or steps we have to take to pray. That line of thinking starts to flirt with religion in the sense that thinking prayer has to follow an exact way every time. When this happens, over time prayer turns into a mundane powerless chore of rambling with no passion, love or fire. And as a matter of fact, Jesus told us about this order of prayer right after he spoke against mindless rambling and constant talking. Prayer is essential to our lives and spiritual growth. It's not just a necessity. It's a privilege and honor that our Creator, our Savior and our Helper craves for us and waits for us to talk and spend time together. I pray we don't keep him waiting.

Our Request, His Will

UNDERSTANDING PRAYER ALLOWS US to peel back the layers on our requests of God. During this time of learning from the Lord, I discovered a couple of truths that are key to getting His intervention and receiving from God. The first step is having a holy desire, and the second is understanding that God has two *"areas"* of His overall will. Let's explore the first step in seeing our prayers manifest, which is that we must have a holy desire. This may seem elementary, but many are surprised by how often some people miss this point. When God began speaking to me about writing this book, he told me, *"So many people have not understood how to receive from me, and the enemy used their confusion to sow seeds of hate, doubt and discontent towards me, which caused some to turn away from me altogether,"* When I heard this, the "Parable of the Sower" that Jesus told in Matthew 13 came to my mind. I wondered how many seeds of faith had been taken by the enemy because their hearts did not understand how to receive from the Lord.

When making a request of God, the Bible makes it clear in many Scriptures that our prayers must be something he accepts for us to have. One of those Scriptures is 1 John 5:14–15 when the Bible says, *"This is the confidence we have in approaching God: that if we ask anything according to His will, he hears us. And since we know he hears us, (whatever we ask) we know that we have what we asked of him."* Focus on the *"according to"* part in this Scripture. These two words are so packed with revelation because they encompass both steps in receiving from the Lord. They can also mean "in agreement with." Our requests must be in agreement with God's will.

I suppose right now someone is saying, "*Well that's obvious, doesn't take a deep thinker to understand that*" and I agree, however it is the small foxes that ruin the vine. Most would agree 100% that asking the Lord to help become a better drug dealer or asking God to let a spouse die to be with another person is completely against His will. But what about the more intricate requests that we think God would approve? For example, what if a person is believing for a new job that on paper looks great, but God, who sees and knows all, understands that this particular position would introduce the person asking for this job to new forms of temptation that this individual is not strong enough to resist. The job might open up to a world of depression, fear and anxiety that God never meant for the person to suffer. This is exactly what happened to me, I lived this once. In my late twenties, I was recruited for a job that offered much more money and had all the perks I could dream of asking. The place I was working at the time paid less money and had other challenges, but I knew I was supposed to be there. I took the other offer without even asking God's input, and that new position almost killed me in many ways with my sanity and mental health being most affected. What we must always remember is that God is a good Father, like all good parents who will not give their children anything that will hurt them in any way.

The second step in receiving from the Lord is understanding that God has two overall *"areas"* of His will. My faith life, in terms of believing God for provision, has been a roller coaster ride. I remember years ago, I came across teachings on faith from pastors like Creflo Dollar, John Osteen and David Brown. Not faith in the sense of my salvation, but rather the faith to believe God for a better life and the ability to have enough to give to others. When I was first introduced to this idea, I was a man on fire, standing on promises and seeing results left and right. But over the years, I got lazy and treated God as a "pushbutton," and drifted into a vending machine mindset where I would only seek him when I wanted something. This led to problems because I needed to rebuild my faith each time I asked God for things, instead of building my faith continually. When it came to having faith for requesting needs from God, I had to "get" ready, instead of "staying" ready. As I alluded to earlier, this caused issues by allowing the enemy to come into my life and sow those weeds of doubt and confusion. My thoughts got so badly mixed up, and I got so confused, that I almost stopped asking God altogether. I thought that if I was believing in something that was not specifically in His will, then he would not hear me, like 1 John 5:14 said he would. And if he had not heard me, I should not be expecting to see my desires in my life. Then God in His grace introduced me to the thinking of His will in two categories of requests: specific and general. I heard a pastor say this one time, and it blew me away, that "God has two sets of wills, he has a general will for your life, and he has a specific will for your life." I now believe it is very important for us to comprehend these two areas of God's will, so we can ask and pursue requests, while managing our expectations appropriately. I always felt the Bible does speak to all issues of life, but what about specifics? For example, if a person has an illness in the body and needs immediate healing, there are iron clad promises that deal specifically with healing. On the other hand, if someone is planning a family vacation and is $1,500 short of having the time of life in fun, does the Bible speak to these types of issues?

The good news is that it does, and even if the Bible doesn't have specific promises to address needs and wants like vacation funds, it does have specific promises like Psalm 37:4 when it talks about God giving us the desires of our hearts. Remembering that the phrase *"according to His will"* in 1 John tackles many requests. Not only can that phrase be translated "in agreement with," but it could also read "run alongside of," so we can rephrase that Scripture in 1 John to say, *"This is the confidence we have in approaching God: that if we ask anything [that runs alongside] His will, he hears us. And since we know he hears us, whatever we ask, we know that he heard what we asked of him."* The amazing point of my revelation is that the Bible talks to my requests specifically, like healing in my physical body *or* general wants that are not verbatim in the

Bible, like the money for a vacation. All my prayer has to do is "run alongside" or "agree" with God's will, then when it does, I can be sure I have what I asked because of the promise in 1 John 5:14–15. Remember, the Word of God is the will of God, and I believe that when we come to God in a general sense, we allow ourselves to trust the Lord with a little "wiggle room" when it comes to how he answers us. If we ever have a question about if our desires and needs agree with His will, then we must go to His Word to find out the truth. This is when a relationship with the Holy Spirit is very important because he will help us see if what we are asking passes the "smell test" with him. In the example I gave about the family vacation, some may say, *"God does not care about things like that,"* or like I used to think, *"He only cares about my salvation, not about my day-to-day life or joy."* However, there are multiple promises in the Bible that speak about him wanting us to have fun, relaxation, and great times. So never be afraid to ask him and seek His will in His Word.

Not only did God show me the steps in receiving from him, but he showed me a way to test or "screen" my requests to be sure they agree with His will following Jeremiah 29:11. Most of us know this Scripture, as it is one of the most used Scriptures for someone graduating or retiring: *"For I know the plans I have for you, plans of peace and not evil, Plans to give you an expected end."* The words "peace" and "evil" in the Scripture mean the following:

Peace:

> safety, completeness, soundness (in body), welfare, health, prosperity, peace, quiet, tranquility, friendship (with God and humans), peace (from war)[1]

---

1. *Peace* English Definition Meaning

Evil:

> bad, unpleasant, wicked actions, misery, calamity, injury, wrong, unhappiness, trouble[2]

Every time we want to see if the desires that we are believing God will provide align with His general will, run them through the *Jeremiah* 29:11 test and see if those desires agree with the "peace" he wants to give us or the "evil" he is against.

Remember that God is a God of His timing. Even if the request isn't what he has for us at the specific time we ask, then *something* will come, regardless, seen or unseen. We can be expectant and excited because no matter what, we know something is going to come from our sincere requests. The answer may not be seen or physical, but it will be what we really desire or what we really need because His Word won't return void.

Remember God is a God Who knows all. Meaning God is not dumb; He knows what we actually need or desire. I have heard people talk about God as if he is out of tune with our needs and desires. However, in Matthew 7:9–10 Jesus said, *"You parents—if your children ask for a loaf of bread, do you give them a stone instead? Or if they ask for a fish, do you give them a snake? Of course not! So if you sinful people know how to give good gifts to your children, how much more will your heavenly Father give good gifts to those who ask him?"* Jesus clearly states here that if our kids are asking for X, we wouldn't give them Z; therefore, God wouldn't give us what we don't need. Furthermore, we can be absolutely confident that the Lord will not withhold any good thing from us. We know that for two reasons: The first reason supports that the Bible outright says this in Psalm 84:1. Secondly, the Bible also points out in Romans that God did not withhold even his son from us, which is the best gift of all. Now, we can be sure that he will graciously give us anything else that is in His will for us because everything pales in comparison to Jesus. It is like if parents gave $100,000 because their children needed it to save their house from being foreclosed,

---

2. *Evil* English Definition and Meaning

and at another time the same child wanted $100 to go out and have fun. The kid knows to ask the parents for the $100 and expects to get it because it is much less than the $100,000 that they gave in the past. The same is with Jesus, we needed him, and God gave Him to us freely. Therefore, anything we can imagine that we could ask, no matter how important or complicated, can never match the gift of Jesus, so we can be confident that he will answer.

At one point, I got in my head the opposite of what Jesus said in Matthew 7, and I thought God would not meet my actual need or desire but would rather give me what I didn't need or desire. Then the Holy Spirit gave me a picture in my head of a man on a boat watching another man flailing around and drowning in the water. While the man drowning was yelling for help, the man on the boat just watched with intense sadness while holding an ice cream cone in one hand and a life jacket in the other.

Then the Lord spoke, *"Now in this situation, would the man on the boat throw the drowning man an ice cream cone knowing he needs a life preserver or flotation device?"* I said, "Of course not, Lord," and he said, *"Neither would I."* Then 1 John 3:17 came to mind where the Bible says, *"If someone has enough money to live well and sees a brother or sister in need but shows no compassion—how can God's love be in that person?"* Then the Lord spoke to me again and said, *"If I am against someone not helping others when they have the ability, then why would I do it? Why would I do the thing I am against?"* I've heard it said that sometimes God will not give us what we ask for, even if it agrees with His will, in order to teach us a lesson. Like a man believing for a new heart represents the drowning man in the picture. God, who is represented as the man in the boat, wouldn't answer the drowning man by giving him only peace to deal with His situation, even though God has the capability to give the drowning man all that he really needs. I will discuss this fully in a later chapter and will show beyond a shadow of a doubt that God is against not supplying answers to our prayers, but for now try to understand the symbolism of the picture.

Lastly, the Lord showed me that when expecting from him, our requests MUST agree with His will, but multiple things can agree with His will at the same time. Remember how I talked about God being the most purposeful Being ever, sometimes we forget this critical point, and we try to put him in a single box. In the past, I learned that I was being too singular in my asking. Case in point, in the Garden of Eden, God told Adam and Eve that they could eat any of the multitude of trees and food sources around. In this example, there were many *general* options that agreed with the *specifics* of God's will, which was for them to eat and be healthy. Again, this will be addressed fully in another chapter but for now just know that God is so vast, we can pursue and expect multiple things from him to answer our desires and needs. So being the faith hounds that we are, I want us to adopt a new philosophy. Let's say to ourselves:

> *I am going to relentlessly pursue the thing I am expecting from God, while believing it agrees with His general will, until he tells me it does not agree with His specific will. If the thing I am pursuing doesn't agree with His will for me, then I know and expect with excitement because he is a good Father, and I know something is coming, and it will be what he has for me, not worse or less than what I asked for.* Thinking like this is how we fight; it's how we win!

Now I would consider it a crime if I didn't make sure to clarify a very important word that people have used to deal with this topic. That word is *sovereign,* and it means that someone has "supreme power and authority." God is sovereign; and in teaching people that their words, faith or works of faith will always manifest what they want when they want it, basically teaches they are more sovereign than God. When this kind of thinking is tolerated, it's a slippery slope leading to thinking people don't need the Lord, and that we are "God" ourselves. Now it is possible for us to force what we want to happen but this should not be the case, and quite frankly, we should not want it this way. If this idea is adopted, we are saying that we know better than God. Earlier, in my example about taking a job without even seeking God's will, I ignored the sovereignty of God, and it almost destroyed me. On the flip side, when we trust him and give him complete authority, he will rule in our lives. The thinking that our faith can somehow overrule God's authority is really based out of fear. It's the fear of "*What if what God wants for me isn't the best?*" The fact is that His plans are higher and better than ours. We can trust Jesus when he said in Matthew 7:8–11 that God won't give us less or worse than what we ask, because God is a good Father Who gives good things. We can boldly cast that fear down and rest in the truth that God is sovereign, and in His sovereignty is good will towards us. The "super Scripture sighting" that addresses this fear of not trusting the Lord's sovereignty and believing that if our requests differ from His will, then he might give less or worse than what we expect can be found in Philippians and Jeremiah. Philippians 4:6 and Jeremiah 29:11, fit perfectly together in this area, because Philippians 4:6 says to be anxious for nothing, and Jeremiah 29:11 says God knows the plans he has towards us. Now, when placing those verses together, the "super Scripture sighting" reads:

"I will be anxious for nothing (Phil 4:6) *because* God's plans for me are of peace and not evil (Jeremiah 29:11)."

This played out in my life in a major way. About six years ago, I was approached about a job for a highly sought-after company in my regional area. The position would have come with more than triple the amount of money that I was currently making, less stress, more time at home and other benefits like those. *Seems great, right?* While waiting for this position, I had learned my lesson about "making" things happen on my own power, and I was right in the middle of this season of learning from the Lord. I allowed him to lead me and train me in receiving wisdom from him, while pursuing this new position. I did not get the job for which I was originally approached, but I was hired for a better one in that same company with more money and incentives. Also, the position I ultimately landed is in an industry where the sky's the limit, there is no cap as to where I can advance. The kicker to this story is that a year after I started in my current position, there was a major shakeup in the area where I was originally recruited. Many employees in that department lost their jobs, and if I had started when the position first opened, I would have likely been one of them. Clearly, when we make room for God's will and His sovereignty, Jeremiah 29:11 jumps off the page, and we see the message work in our lives. We see that God really does have plans for us, and they are of good and not of evil!

Before I close this chapter, I want to take a step back and give more clarification on exactly what I meant when talking about God's sovereignty. Several doctrines and schools of thought believe some dangerous ideas about the Lord's sovereignty. They claim God has the right to go against His own promises at times just because he mysteriously wants to. God tells us in Malachi 3:6, "*I AM the Lord, I change not.*" I believe that when a prayer is not answered in the way or time we ask, it's a hang up on our end from praying "amiss" or in doubt. God is sovereign in that he is King: His rules and authority apply to everyone equally, and His sovereignty does not override His integrity, truthfulness, or faithfulness to fulfill His promises. Earlier I talked about how we should not force our will to trump God's rule in our life. However, this does not mean the Lord will not move out of our way and allow us to "make things happen" for ourselves like in the example I shared taking a job that almost ruined me. I have heard it taught like this for years, "God is a gentleman, and will not force himself on anyone." He will not overpower us and give us what we do not ask for, even if it seems a good thing. For example, Hell was never intended for us. The Lord does not want one person to go there and be eternally separated from him. However, he has made us all free–will agents, so even though he does not want people to go, because of their own actions and lack of faith in Jesus, some will die and go to hell. God will not use His will to trump ours for any reason. Furthermore, he is not a "will violator" meaning that he will not overtake one person's will to answer another person's prayer. For example, say someone is praying for a specific job at a company. They pray, "Lord I want Mr. Smith to hire me specifically." In actuality, Mr. Smith has his own will and thoughts, so should we expect God to overpower Mr. Smith and totally disregard what he wants? Remember, we serve

OUR REQUEST, HIS WILL

an eternal God who has infinite possibilities to answer our prayers. Now someone reading this may disagree with what I just said. Some may use God delivering Egypt from slavery as an example of God overriding an individual's will, but this is still incorrect. Yes, it was Pharaoh's "will" for Israel to stay in captivity; however, the Lord gave multiple opportunities for Pharaoh to change his will. Even though he refused many times, he came to the point that the consequences of his refusal to change his will wore him down, and Pharaoh finally gave in to God's will. If God wanted, he could have just snatched His people out of Egypt, regardless of Pharaoh's wants. Again, being the gentleman that God is, he gave ample time for Pharaoh to change his thinking and repent.

Faith Hound... The Pursuit

I WENT THROUGH A time in my life where I experienced the Lord's "*No*" on quite a few requests, that taught me many lessons. One of the things he showed was that over time I had become lazy, and quite frankly, weak in my faith life. I would say to myself, "*I'm not going to believe God for anything unless I know it's His will.*" This is still true to a degree, but if we are not careful that mentality can turn into a crutch causing us to not pursue anything at all. I have shown how my mind works; I am very much a visual person, and wisdom finds its mark in my mind when it's delivered via pictures and illustrations. The entire premise of this book was actually derived from this chapter. In the last chapter, I talked about how I was a man on fire when I was first introduced to faith and began receiving from the Lord. I'm telling you, readers; it was a passion I can't describe, and then my faith rocketed when the manifestations actually showed in my life! In my mind, I saw the promises of God as a fox or wild game, and my faith was a ravenous, relentless hound who at the moment his Master said, "Go," it took off and chased the fox down, completely devouring it. I know this is rough imagery but let me explain. I was so "gung-ho" about God's promises and their manifestations that I just went after them with my ears pinned back and unabashed. Imagine a prisoner who had been in jail his whole life, and after many years was let out and told to go get his life back! But as time passed, I became a complacent, timid, lazy, sleepy teacup yorkie, instead of the excited passionate Labrador I once was.

Faith Hound ... The Pursuit

From then to now, I have expanded my thinking from that one "hound" to three different types of "hounds" that people can think, and act, like in their faith lives. The first type of faith hound says: *"Unless I know it's here, I will not pursue with faith."*

This type of faith is not really faith at all. Because knowing with some sort of tangible proof, means not even needing faith. Knowledge does not need faith because it has physical evidence. This is the type of faith hound that is lazy and not moving at all. In fact, if your dog acted like this type of faith hound you would call his name and have pet him just to make sure he is even alive.

The Lord showed me how, like most, I started like this type of faith hound. I was always looking for physical proof that what I was believing was happening. If we see something is here, then there is no need to use faith. That is not a sacrilegious thing to say, it's just the truth. For instance, I do not need to use my faith that I have a home. Because as I type this chapter, I am sitting in my office at my house. I already have physical, tangible proof of the house, and there is no need to "believe" for it, just the need to be thankful for it.

Another key point the Lord showed was that he is not going to provide anything that will take our faith away from him and His

Faith Hounds

promises. I mean that when I was in this frame of mind, I secretly wanted these physical signs that my desire was coming, so I could attach my faith to those signs, instead of to God's Word. It's easy to expect something, if we know it is coming by physical sight, *but it's entirely different and more pleasing to God when we expect what he promised by faith, without tangible proof.*

The second type of faith hound is a slight improvement from the first because that person says: "*I will not pursue with faith until God tells me to go after it.*" This hound doesn't necessarily need physical proof to believe, however it wants his master to show his approval in the desired request. So this hound is attentive and ready to go but it still isn't in pursuit of anything.

This kind of thinking is acceptable and perfectly biblical. To seek God before spending energy in pursuit of His promises is right. David asked God in 2 Samuel 5:19, "*Shall I go after them?*" when he was pursuing the Philistines. The trap to watch for is if we fail to actively seek God's will over the request and say, "*I have faith, but I'm waiting on the Lord to show me.*" If the faith we say we have isn't backed by the work of seeking His will, then our faith is "dead." In other words, saying we're waiting to see if the desire agrees with God's will is fine, but we need to have faith he will lead us to what he wants, while we back that faith by actively pursuing wisdom.

The Lord told me long ago, "*you say you will not pursue and believe until you know. Well, I say unless you pursue, you will not find out.*" Another way to look at this is when the world says "No," but God says "Yes!" The Bible says that the kingdom suffers violence, and the violent takes it by force. The Word of God is not encouraging violence here at all, but it is talking about taking what God has for us in the faith realm. If we are not actively pursuing the wisdom we need, then we won't know whether the "No" we face about our prayers is from the world or from God. If it's a "No" from the world, then it can be overtaken by faith! We must get to the point where our active chase is the tangible proof of our faith that the Lord will show us what he wants for us.

I was this second type of faith hound at times. Even when I was not looking for "physical" signs of my manifestation, I would say to myself, "*I'm not going to pursue with my faith towards this thing until I know it's God's will.*" While this kind of thinking is normal, if it is used in the correct context, I was lazy about searching God's will, and afraid that "*what if it does not come?*" and "*it may be a waste of time to even pursue this thing.*" This finally led to altogether doubting God would even tell me if my desire was aligned with His will. The Lord in His grace and patience worked on my heart and showed me the pitfalls to my thinking.

He showed me in His Word found in:

- Hebrews 11:6 when the Bible plainly tells how God is a rewarder of those who *diligently* seek *him*. So, no diligent seeking = no reward.

Faith Hounds

- James 1:5–8 speaks on the promise of God's help. The Amplified Version says, *"He loves to help."* If I doubted His willingness to lead me, then I can forget about seeing the answer.

- Matthew 7: 9–11 Remember Jesus talks about how if humans won't give kids a snake when they ask for fish or a stone when they ask for bread, then how much more does God give good gifts to those who ask. So I drew the conclusion that I can pursue the desire I am believing for with reckless abandon, because no matter what, God is not going to give me worse or less than what I asked of him.

Earlier, I made the case that our faith cannot trump God's sovereignty. I shared how God gave me a better job than the one I originally thought he had for me. Being this type of faith hound, we can't sit on our hands, or paws I guess would be appropriate for this application, and adopt the thinking, *"I will not pursue unless I know,"* and then do nothing to actually find out if it's his will. If I had not pursued the job that I thought he planned for me, then I would not have gained the one he actually manifested for me, which was better.

Finally, the last type of faith hound says: *"I will be completely sold out, and relentlessly pursue the request I am believing, until my Master tells me it doesn't agree with his specific will for me."*

48

Faith Hound ... The Pursuit

We can only be this type of faith hound if we are void of that "*what if*" fear. Completely destroying the "*I could be wasting my time*" mentality. Replacing these thoughts with the trust that, no matter what, God is going to give us something, and it's going to be what we need at the perfect time. Thankfully, this is where I am now in my faith life. This relentless, excited and active faith hound. The type of believer who ravenously pursues and hunts down all that God has for me, and also for my family, my friends, and my church, while trusting my Master to redirect me, when necessary. Always expecting in full faith that if the desire I am after isn't what he wants, then what he actually desires for me must be much better, because of the revelation the Lord showed me in 1 Peter.

In 1 Peter 1:7, the Bible preaches how precious our faith is to God, and it's more important to him than gold. I will never forget when the Lord taught me this as he whispered to my heart, "*Now son, when was the last time you have ever seen gold discarded or thrown away?*" I said, "Well never, Lord," and he answered as plain as day, "*Exactly, so don't ever be afraid thinking what if I pursue and nothing happens or think any faith you spend on a prayer is a waste of time, because I will never disregard your faith, but I may redirect it.*"

I am not sure that any of you have ever seen a hunting dog in action. If so, it is one of the most impressive sights that a person will ever see. To witness an animal so in tune with its master, going where his master said to go. I once was invited on a quail hunt where my friend was working some new puppies he was training as bird dogs. During the hunt, we came upon a covey of the quail, and the trained dog sat right at the owner's side, pointing like a pro. You could have drawn a straight line from the tip of the hound's tail to its nose. When we came to the covey, my friend simply said, "Fetch em' up boy," and the dog took off to scatter the quail. During the flurry of wings, feathers and noise, the hound was solely focused on the commands from his master. The owner would say "left" or "right," and the animal would hear him and respond. This is how we have to be, but God does not see us as dogs or animals, in case that was what some might be thinking. When I say words like "master" and "owner," do not let pride slip in by thinking you are no slave to anyone, because I have got news for you. If you have not repented of sin and turned to following Jesus, you are a slave, my friend . . . a slave to sin. We have to be like these hounds; we have to go where our Lord says to go, when he says, because when we allow him to redirect our faith, I am convinced and know from personal experience, that a greater blessing is there waiting for us: One that we can never imagine!

> *Now to the one who is able to do exceeding abundantly above all that we ask or think, according to the power that works in us . . . (Ephesians 3:2)*

The Wait and Expectation

I SEE MOST THINGS in life as a process, and so far, we have covered the bulk of what I view as the most important steps we must take to see our prayers go from conception in our hearts, to actually making the request and finally to manifestation. We have covered:

1. Making sure our relationship with God is real and based on the faith in Christ Jesus and his truth.
2. Understanding that God's promises are in the spirit first and how they manifest in the physical where we exist.
3. Now that we are in Christ, we must follow him, and by doing so, we are guaranteed our requests when they align with his will.
4. Actually making our requests to God.
5. Pursuing God's promises with faith.

Now we have come to the part most of us do not like: the wait and expectation.

While in the process of making special metals and materials, there are two common themes that must take place. With gold for example, there must be fire, high heat and pressure. This is why the Bible talks about how our faith will come out as pure gold after it has been tested. With diamonds, it takes pressure and time before it becomes valued as a precious gem. Our faith for our prayer requests and the manifestations are no different than these treasured materials. Now this begs the two questions that we all have. The first, "*Lord! How long do I have to wait?*" and the second, "*What do I do while waiting?*" Before I dig into the answers, I want us to write down this phrase, *"If our soil is good, then we do not have to worry about when harvest is coming because God is faithful."* If the soil of our hearts is right with God, then the first question of how long it will take is irrelevant because it is completely case by case. At times, I believe our faith can dictate time, but I will discuss this in another chapter.

In the whole process from the desire being in our heart to us asking for it to manifest is all situational; however, we must look at this "wait" period through the eyes of God. The Bible says that to God, a thousand days are like one day, and one day is like a thousand years. This is a simple metaphor to show that God does not view time as we do. He is Alpha and Omega, which means that while he is the beginning of everything, he is also the end of everything, simultaneously. We serve a God who understands our relationship with time and how we view time. Hebrews 4:15 says, *"For we have not a high priest, who cannot be touched with the feeling of our infirmities; but was in all points tempted like as we are, yet without sin."* Jesus understands our dependency on time because he lived among us. Furthermore, remember God created our concept of time when he created day and night, because inside of that concept are seconds, minutes and hours. Some things are instant manifestations, and others not so instant. Another aspect of viewing our manifestation from God's point of view is seeing like he does in the sense that we already have manifestation of requests, when we first asked, as previously discussed.

It's so interesting to me that we can study the same Scripture over and over, and every time, we will get new revelation. It's like biting into a nice ribeye steak, and every bite tastes as delicious as the first. Mark 11:24 is one of these Scriptures when Jesus said, *"Therefore I tell you, whatever you ask for in prayer, believe that you have received it, and it will be yours."* The first part of this Scripture is the faith aspect of our prayer lives, while the end speaks to the manifestation. Notice that Jesus keeps it open-ended by saying, "*it will be yours,*" without committing to a time frame. This is why I said our manifestations are case by case. For example, when people pray the "Prayer of Salvation," and they ask the Lord to forgive them and wash them clean with his Blood, the answer to that prayer is obviously, "Yes," and they have salvation at that point. But the "manifestation" of that eternal life will not show until each person has passed away in the flesh. On the flip side of that coin, we all have had times when our prayer manifested years, days, hours or minutes after we prayed.

A pastor explained this to me by showing the entire prayer process follows God's law of *seed*, *time* and then *harvest*. We know well about the seed and harvest portion of this equation; however, the *time* part is where we often stumble. This law must take place in every principle of life. Take the salvation example I gave. Each person of the "lost" group had the "seed" of the gospel planted in their hearts at some point. It could have been right before they made the decision to give their lives to the Lord, or it could have been planted when they were five years old, and their grandmother always talked to them about Jesus. Now at thirty-five years old, they made the decision and prayed. In that case, the "time" aspect was thirty years, and then came the "harvest."

The second question we all have asked ourselves when expecting an answer to prayer is, "*What do we do while we wait?*" This is perhaps the most important of the questions because it is the "what" we do while we wait that paves the way for manifestation, but it's also the easiest to answer. We wait, and we expect! Inside our expectation is the work we do to grow and show our faith in God that makes our faith alive. There is a reason why the Bible compares our prayers and faith to seeds. First, it's a great visualization, and second, a plant seed goes through the exact same process our faith goes through from planting to harvest. I already hit on the "time" portion of the process, but we must look at the "time" portion just like a farmer does, while his seed is in the ground. *What does a farmer do while he waits?* He expects a crop to grow, and he shows the expectation by the work of preparing the ground for the plants' manifestation. *How can we do this with our faith seeds when we are expecting our breakthrough?*

Faith Hounds

In the book of James, the Bible says that *"faith with no works is dead."* This is a staple of the Christian faith, and most of us have heard it said or read. However, what are these "works" that make our faith alive and thriving? Again, this is a case-by-case situation. If people are believing for financial breakthroughs, their "works" will be different from people who may be believing for spouses. For the financial breakthrough, people should not stop generosity in giving to others, even if they may not seem to have enough material resources, but they will still bless others how they can with what they have. On the other hand, to those believing for spouses, they will back their faith in God's Word over the situation by "works" of keeping themselves pure sexually, being friendly to people and seeking God's guidance. The number one priority I have found that we all must do, and I can't emphasize this enough, is no matter what we ask of God and expect to come, we must be Kingdom-minded!

When the Holy Spirit began to teach me these things, he showed me where my thinking was off track. Originally, I was under the impression that my thoughts equaled my faith, and that if I was not actively thinking about my prayers, then manifestation would not happen. I thought that if I was not thinking about my prayers, then God would forget what I was asking from him. This then led to the issue of a limited prayer life. In fact, I would only pray about one request at a time, because I could only focus on one thing at a time. But the Lord in his grace and patience showed me this was flawed thinking. He taught me that even if we forget about what we asked, he will never forget. In Isaiah 49:15-16, the Amplified Bible version says:

> [The Lord answered] Can a woman forget her nursing child and have no compassion on the son of her womb? Even these may forget, but I will not forget you. Indeed, I have inscribed [a picture of] you on the palms of my hands; your city walls are continually before me.

The writer draws a fantastic parallel here to drive this point home. He says that even in the unlikely event a human woman forgets her child, God will not forget us. When I learned this, I was released to literally pray and believe for all sorts of requests and petitions without the self-made shackles of praying for one thing at a time because I could only continually think of one thing at a time. This then led to the realization of where my mind should be all the time, even in the midst of waiting for my prayers to manifest.

Another awesome lesson I have learned while following the Lord is that he will never take something from us or out of us without filling that vacancy with something from him. This was never more evident in this situation, when he took my old thinking out and showed me where I need to be focusing instead. In Matthew 6:33, Jesus said, *"But seek first his kingdom and his righteousness, and all these things will be given to you as well."* The word "seek" here can also mean to *strive after, aim for* or *crave,* so we are to literally strive after, aim for and crave God's Kingdom! *What does that look like, one may ask?* Simply put, it's going after his Kingdom by learning how to live as a Christian, and then advancing his Kingdom by witnessing and winning the "lost." Jesus promises that if we seek the Kingdom first and foremost, if we crave it and demand it in our lives, then all the other things we are praying for will be given to us by default.

I touched on this in a previous chapter, and in the book of 1 Kings, Solomon became the "poster child" for this idea in the Bible. God told Solomon to ask for whatever he wanted. Solomon then asked for one simple thing; he asked for wisdom to lead God's people. In response to Solomon's answer, the Bible says:

> *The Lord was pleased that Solomon had asked for this. So God said to him, "Since you have asked for this and not for long life or wealth for yourself, nor have asked for the death of your enemies but for discernment in administering justice, I will do what you have asked. I will give you a wise and discerning heart, so that there will never have been anyone like you, nor will there ever be. Moreover, I will give you what you have not asked for—both wealth and honor—so that in your lifetime you will have no equal among kings. And if you walk in obedience to me and keep my decrees and commands as David your Father did, I will give you a long life.*

Faith Hounds

With this "blank check" from God, the King asked for wisdom to do right by God's people, which is being Kingdom-minded because it's Kingdom business. As a result, Solomon got a thousand times more than he could have imagined making him the richest man to have ever walked the earth.

I believe this image God put in my heart sums up this truth perfectly.

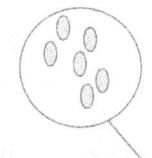

My Old Way of Thinking:

The individual dots are things I thought would not happen if I was not thinking about them constantly.

My New Way of Thinking:

The circle is Matthew 6:33 encompassing the individual things I wanted. While being Kingdom minded like Jesus said, all the other things will fit inside and will come by default.

When our hearts and minds are focused on God's Kingdom first, all the other things we may be praying about will come also.

It is important to understand the difference between a wait versus a delay. I personally do not believe delays are of God, because when we look at a delay, it is a time that something was supposed to be but is held back for some reason. For example, suppose a person needed to be at work at 8:00 a.m. but got stopped at a car wreck site that redirected traffic. When finally getting to work, that person said, "I'm sorry, I was delayed because of the wreck." Although supposed to be there at a certain time, the person was delayed by the wreck. God is never late or delayed in his timing. I do believe God may have us wait at times, because a wait means that something has to take place before another thing happens. If a woman gets pregnant, there is a nine month wait before an average birth, because there are many things that need to happen in the baby's development before the baby arrives fully ready to live. When we evaluate our situation, we have to determine if it's a delay on our part, or a Godly wait. If it's the former, then we have

The Wait and Expectation

to humble ourselves and ask the Lord, "*Ok Jesus, what needs to be done first?*" Another way to consider this idea is how the Bible says that our steps are "*ordered by the Lord.*" If we experience a wait until manifestation, then it is very possible God sent the wait, since he ordered our steps that way.

Waiting is a two-prong situation. Most people "wait" by sitting back with hands folded expecting something to show up. However, biblical waiting is backed by works; otherwise, the faith we are using for manifestation is dead and useless. Waiting is defensive. We have to protect our seeds that are in the ground. If we just planted fresh Bermuda grass seed in our yards, what would we do if as soon as we turn away, there were hundreds of birds eating our seed? After all that work, are we going to just let the birds have our seeds? *No!* The same is true in the faith realm: The birds represent demons and wicked spirits trying to kill our manifestation. I have learned over the years that the enemy has plenty of tactics he employs to do this, but it seems his favorite is to be very covert and sneaky. Instead of making an obvious move to take what is ours, he covertly attacks by sowing seeds of his own in our minds and hearts. He plants what I call, "what if" seeds. Now we have to be careful with these types of seeds because on the surface they look harmless, but they are masked to blend in disguise with righteous seeds. We have all seen them. O sure we have, these seeds are presented to us in thoughts like "*being rational*" or "*faith is fine, but I have to live in the real world.*" Please understand that I am not talking about going to the extreme as some people think. I do believe that God gives us wisdom and discernment for a reason. For example, if anyone is sick, I believe taking the medicine until total healing comes. But there is a fine line that is easily crossed while we are waiting for manifestation. This "*what if*" seed is a tricky one, because it seems like a reasonable truth. I mean, "*Yeah, what if the thing you are expecting in faith does not come or come in time?*" This is a legitimate concern, and I will go further in depth in another chapter, but for now, I learned to turn that "*what if*" question the enemy likes to throw in my face back at him, and this is how we do it.

Faith Hounds

I will never forget the day the Holy Spirit spoke to my heart saying, *"Expectation turns into anxiety when you allow yourself to start considering the alternatives over God's Promises."* In James 1:5–8, the Bible promises that if we want God to lead us, he will, gladly. However, these verses also warn that if we doubt his willingness to help, then we are unstable in all our ways and should not think we will get anything from the Lord. A prime example of this was Peter when he saw Jesus on the water and told Jesus to call him out of the boat. Peter was doing fine walking on the water's surface, until he started looking at the waves and considering the alternative of him sinking over Jesus' promise of protection. The minute he did this, anxiety and fear came over Peter causing him to sink. In our own lives, Peter taking his focus off Jesus and putting it on his surroundings is the same thing we do. We start considering *"what if"* our prayer does not manifest, and the alternative happens. Another example may be a person believing for a financial breakthrough, and the alternative for them not getting it is losing their home. Even though this is a real concern and a possibility, they must not give this thought one centimeter of space to grow in their mind and heart.

In Isaiah 40:31, God makes an amazing promise regarding what happens while we wait. The King James Version says, *"But they that wait upon the Lord shall renew their strength; they shall mount up with wings as eagles; they shall run, and not be weary; and they shall walk, and not faint."* Notice there is a guarantee here along with a stipulation. The guarantee is that we gain strength when we execute the stipulation: We wait on the Lord. Not on the government, not on our neighbor, not on our jobs. But wait on the Lord! This is just another example of the sustenance of God that we have seen already. While we wait, God will sustain us with all we need, including strength and stamina.

Remember that being the faith hounds who trust God to redirect our faith is how we completely destroy the *"what if"* seed. When the enemy starts to bark, we faith hounds need to bark back by saying, *"Devil, the only 'what if' I will consider is a wise one for discernment that can show if what I am asking for aligns with God's*

will. And Jeremiah 29:11 declares, 'His plans for me are of peace and NOT evil.' Also, according to Isaiah 55:8, God's thoughts are higher than mine, so if he is redirecting my faith, he is redirecting it to something beyond better than what I could think or ask! He promised that he will never disregard my faith, but he may redirect it: I trust him!"
My friend, this is how we fight . . . and break the enemy's back!

Resting

MAKE NO MISTAKE, MY friends, while waiting and expecting manifestations to our prayers, we have roles to play and work to do. Our primary focus should be on God's Kingdom during this time, so now I want to dive deeper into what we can do during our wait time. Many people, like me, have a problem just sitting still. Every time I have some down time, I almost always think of other activities that I could be doing. One activity we can do while we wait for manifestations: We can rest. When reading the word "rest," it may conjure images of a vacation or someone on the beach having a pink drink with an umbrella sticking out of it. This is not the type of rest I am talking about for this waiting time. From the first prayer until final manifestation, we rest in faith, while fighting in faith. Let me explain what biblical resting is, what resting isn't and how to rest.

What Resting Is:

True resting in God's promises is working and fighting to stay in faith. The Bible says this perfectly in Ephesians 6:13–17:

> *Wherefore take unto you the whole armor of God that ye may be able to withstand in the evil day, and having done all, to stand. Stand therefore, having your loins girt about with truth, and having on the breastplate of righteousness; And your feet shod with the preparation of the gospel of peace; Above all, taking the shield of faith, wherewith ye*

shall be able to quench all the fiery darts of the wicked. And take the helmet of salvation, and the sword of the Spirit, which is the word of God.

So, after doing all we can, the Word says to stand and suit ourselves for a fight. God knew that we would certainly see a fight when we are expecting manifestation in our lives. Furthermore, he knew the waiting time would be arduous for us at times. That's why in Galatians 6:9 the Bible says, *"And let us not be weary in well doing: for in due season we shall reap, if we faint not."*

Resting is also keeping focus on the Lord and his Word. I already discussed this when I spoke about Peter, when the only time he began to sink was taking his eyes off Jesus and started looking at the storm instead. Remember that we are in for a fight when we start believing God will answer our prayer. The enemy will try to stop our manifestation for a multitude of reasons: his hate for God's children and his effort to deter others from having faith when they see our answers being manifested to name a few. We will be under constant attack from the enemy, but the good news is that our living Savior, when he was on the Cross, already defeated the enemy. Satan has no power over us. We will have to fight to stay in faith and keep the peace that Jesus gives.

During our resting, the Bible highlights the power of our mouths with everything that praise, worship, and the aspect of confessing God's promises will do. Many of us have heard people refer to this in another way called "power of the words." There is indeed a great deal of power in what we say. Besides what the Bible says about our words, the power of our words is prevalent in every area of our lives. Some may call this, "positive self-talk" or "inner affirmation," but at the end of the day, this is a principle God laid down before humans put their spin on it. My grandmother knew this power. I remember when I was a kid, she loved yellow roses and had a beautiful garden full of them. These flowers were enormous and beautiful, so I asked her one day, "Granny, why are your flowers so pretty when your neighbors' flowers are not?" She smiled and said, "O that's because Granny sings and talks nice to her flowers." As she watered those roses, I remember her going to each one and humming some melody, then she would say something kind to each flower. Like my Granny knew, here are some truths to the power of speaking God's word.

- Angels hearken and come at God's Word *(Dan 10:12; Psalm 103:20)*.
  - *Hearken, in Psalm 103, means to listen or regard, so the angels are listening for the Word of God to come out of our mouths. Proof of this is in Daniel when the Bible records that the Angel told Daniel from the first day Daniel prayed that he was heard. However, how can the angels listen for something that isn't even being spoken?*
- We will answer for idle, lazy words that work. So, our words need to be active *(Matt 12:36)*.
  - *The word idle here means "lazy" or "unemployed." So, our words are to work and work towards God's will.*
- What we say can bring life or death *(Prov 18:21)*.
  - *Our words hold the power of speaking life into a situation; they also have the power to speak death.*
- God's Word is active, powerful and alive *(Heb 4:12)*.
  - *God's Word is a sharp sword. Cutting going into the world when we speak it. But I ask, how can his Word be active, if it is not released?*
- God is watching over his Word to perform it *(Jer 1:12)*.
  - *The Lord is not a liar, so he watches over his Word to do as promised when it is released in accordance with his will. Why would he perform his will if his Word isn't being released?*
- What we say shows what's in our hearts *(Luke 6:45; 2 Cor 4:13)*.
  - *Our words are the mirror to show what we believe.*

- When we decree, his Word will be done *(Job 22:28)*.
  - *This is the power God has given us, that our words come to pass. As long as they agree and run alongside his will.*

This is the "super Scripture sighting" I found about the power of speaking God's Word:

"If we ask anything according to his will, he hears us (1 John 5:14). He hears us *because,* he is looking for his word (Jeremiah 1:12). "And since he hears us, we know we have what we asked for, (John 5:15). *We have it because,* once he sees his word, he does it, (Jeremiah 1:12)."

Hebrews 4:12 calls the spoken Word of God sharper than any two-edged sword. A two-edged sword cuts going in and cuts coming out. When we speak God's Word and make confessions that align with his will, then those words cut going into the spirit and physical world, and they cut coming out, when the promise manifests out of the spirit into the physical.

Another point I will make about the power of our words is to remember we have been given command and the authority to bind and loose the enemy's ability over our lives. The Bible tells us something I find chilling about the power of our words in Numbers 14. In Numbers 14:28, God said to Moses, *"Say unto them, 'As truly as I live,' saith the Lord, 'as ye have spoken in mine ears, so will I do to you.'"* He said this in response to Israel complaining and speaking negatively. Other translations say, *". . . as I heard the words out of their mouth, that will I do."* God and the angels are listening to our very words. In the case of the Israelites, their words of negativity worked against them as God keeps his Word.

When we look at the power of our words, our works of faith, and our resting, while we wait for manifestation, we may not see the correlation between these three roles. However, there is a strong link, because after we have done all we can to make sure that what we are believing is in line with God's will, it is what we do in that waiting period that sets the table for harvest or disaster.

FAITH HOUNDS

What Resting Isn't:

Another key aspect to remember is that biblical resting is not rest from works of faith. Resting is not kicking our feet up and interlocking our fingers behind our heads saying, "Alright Lord, I am ready for my answer." At this point in the book, it should be very clear, as the book title states, we have to be relentless while going after the promises of God. The Word of God says that if a man does not work, he will not eat, and I believe that speaks to the spiritual, too. If we don't have works to show our real faith in God, then like James says, that faith we claim we have is dead. Only living faith sees the sick healed; only living faith sees the dead rise; only living faith can save our souls; and only living faith will bring our manifestations! Furthermore, the resting and the power of our words that we confess while waiting to see our prayers answered are key. I'm not talking about a powerless repetition of Scripture that gets the job done. Jesus spoke against this when he talked about how to pray. I'm talking about the power of our confession that agrees with what God said about the situation. Remember our words are only effective when they first agree with what God said, and second, are based in real faith in what God said. Also, it's important to be sure not to let our words be thought of as the power that brought manifestation. This can easily happen because they can be heard, so they are tangible. But it is the heart behind the words that God sees.

How To Rest:

I have shared what resting is and isn't, so now let's look at some ways to actually rest. There is a comic strip that shows a person talking to a friend saying, "Jim, I'm depressed." In the next drawing his friend, Jim, says, "Well, stop it, Tony!" Then in the third picture the depressed man, Tony, is shown hitting his head while saying, "Man, why didn't I think about that." I don't know about anyone else, but it infuriates me when people try to give some basic advice to a complicated situation. Granted, that basic information they give could be important, but likely already known to the person with the problem. The same is true in this area of how to rest. In my experience, it is not as simple as just not thinking about the prayer we are wanting answered, and it sure as sugar isn't that easy to just not "worry" about it, like many of our friends try to advise us. Otherwise, like Tony, we all would slap our heads and say, "Well, why didn't I think of that!"

The first thing we have to do when trying to enter into a period of rest is to believe we have received it already, and that it's already on the way. We already searched into Scripture and found 2 Peter 1:3 and Mark 11:24 are both fundamental to believe when we begin our rest period. Like Mark 11:24 encourages, believing that God has already said "Yes" to our requests and desires paves the way for peace. If people work for a good company and have never had an issue with payroll, then they likely have full confidence and trust that their wages will be deposited in their accounts when it's time. If their kids come to them and ask for dinner, they know with full trust they will be fed, because their parents love them, and their request is a vital need for their lives. We know if our requests of God pertain to life and godliness, like 2 Peter 1:3 tells us, then we know those requests are in the bag, so we can rest in that knowledge.

Secondly, when it comes to the execution of resting, it's important to give the issue over to the Lord and allow him to keep control of that time. Not to belabor the point I made in the chapter titled *Prayer*, " . . . we are told to cast our cares over to the Lord for a reason in 1 Peter 5:7." Notice there is no mention about casting our cares to him for a week, and then picking up those cares again. I struggle with this area: I will give a certain thing over to the Lord, but over time, I find myself taking it back by trying to "manage" it on my own. First Corinthians goes as far to say that we are co-laborers with God, we are not His boss. Also, giving our cares over to the Lord is not without invitation either. Matthew 11:28 says, *"Come to me, all you who are weary and burdened, and I will give you rest."* Jesus tells us to come to him, and then he promises we will get his rest in return. Finally, to prove God does not want us worrying or being anxious, Jesus tells us in James 14:27, *"Peace I leave with you; my peace I give you. I do not give to you as the world gives. Do not let your hearts be troubled and do not be afraid."*

My whole life, after we have a huge meal at my Uncle Morris' house, he has said, "Nephew, if you leave here and you're still not full with all this food around, it's your fault." That's the same in this area of rest, if at this point, we still refuse to give the issue and expectation over to the Lord after all the promises of encouragement, peace, and rest, then it's our fault.

Lastly, I have learned what we can do daily while resting. What I have shared so far is a high-level overview, but what about the day-to-day nitty gritty? Most people are like me; we want and need something we can literally do, otherwise we feel useless. I call this area "Daily Living" in Jesus using what I have learned that I should be doing all the time, but especially during times of rest:

Be Kingdom-Minded:

The Kingdom of God should be our primary focus by thinking of ways to advance it, like sharing the gospel with others and building the Kingdom in our own lives by how we live and follow the Lord.

Be a Faith Builder:

Faith comes by hearing the Word. Every time we ingest God's Word, we are building and fortifying our faith by making it strong for when the enemy inevitably attacks.

Be a Worshiper:

Worship is a two-pronged weapon. First, it is intimate and allows us to give God what he craves, which is to spend time with us. Second, our worship is a form of warfare. It can be used to let the Lord build a stronghold against the enemy and cause whatever the enemy is trying to do to us to fail.

RESTING

Be a Prayer Warrior in The Spirit and In The Natural:

Remember, when we pray, we are asking the Lord to intercede on our behalf.

When we pray in the spirit, we are:

- Speaking directly to God–directly from our spirit to his–and our spirits are being built up (1 Corinthians 14:2–4).
- Allowing the Holy Spirit to intercede for us in accordance with God's will (Romans 8:26–27).

Be a Seed Sower:

Sow seeds of the Kingdom every day, into ourselves and others.

Be a Thinker:

Every day, take time to think about the Lord and what he did for us: Not just salvation, but everything, from small intimate answers to our prayers all the way to the big miracles that have manifested.

Guard Your Heart:

Another action we need to do while resting is to guard our hearts. I will speak on the enemy's plans and how he attacks later in the book, but for now I will highlight one of the main strategies Satan employs while we're resting. He attacks our thoughts because our thinking is the highway to our hearts, and our hearts are where our faith resides. The Bible says to guard our hearts for a reason, because out of our hearts come the issues of life. Picture your heart being surrounded by a big beautifully ornate castle. With guards on the top and a big draw bridge over a deep moat:

Faith Hounds

Now picture a little lone rider on the other side of the moat trying to get in. This rider represents the attack of the enemy.

It could be blatantly obvious that this thought is from the enemy, when we know the thoughts that popped into our heads are bad. Sometimes, and more often than not, the enemy is more subtle and tricky. The thought is dressed as a Trojan horse and looks like it's the truth waiting for you to lower the draw bridge and gain entry. Sometimes, it's dressed up in half-truths or even facts out of context. It's important that we understand the difference between the truth and facts. Facts are important, and are not to be ignored, but the facts of the issue aren't the whole story. In the lens of the pictures above, think of this example. A person with cancer is resting in God's promise for healing and guarding his heart while believing God and waiting for healing to manifest. A thought aka "rider" shows up wanting to gain entry inside this person's mind and heart. This thought says, *"You have cancer; it cannot be healed, and there is no cure."* The "rider," dressed up in facts, wants inside this person's heart to steal his faith. It's tempting to let this "rider" in because it is a fact that some forms of cancer that afflict people have no known cure. But even though the information about cancer may be a fact, the thought of the enemy is not the truth. The truth is what God said about the matter, which is by his stripes, we are healed. This "rider" seemed right, but the man, being a faith hound, is relentlessly pursuing the healing promises of God. He finds out the truth over the fact and does not give this "rider," this Trojan horse, thought entry to his castle (his mind), thus protecting his heart. We must be mindful to guard our hearts and stay in constant contact with the Lord by allowing him to always lead us, especially during our rest, and by letting him show us if the thoughts we have are from him or the enemy.

As I have said before, I have learned from God that he will never take something away or out of us without replacing it with something from him. This belief is also true for our thoughts. Jesus made this known when he explained in Matthew 12:43–45 what happens when an unclean spirit is cast out of a person. The unclean spirit goes out and brings in seven more spirits that are even stronger than it is. When the unclean spirit returns to the person, it finds its "home," as Jesus states, empty, clean and put in order, so the person is worse off than before the one unclean spirit was removed, because the person now has more unclean spirits tormenting him, seven of which are more powerful than the original one the person had.

In this story, Jesus is not only talking about our spiritual lives, but also our thought lives. This makes it extremely important that we do not fall for the worldly thinking of "positive self-talk" or "self-meditation" that is not founded on the Word of God. It's true that we can try to clean up our lives and get things in order, but if that void space is not filled with Jesus, then we will be worse off than we were. God knew this, and in his wisdom, he left us instruction in Philippians 4:8, *"Finally, brethren, whatsoever things are true, whatsoever things are honest, whatsoever things are just, whatsoever things are pure, whatsoever things are lovely, whatsoever things are of good report; if there be any virtue, and if there be any praise, think on these things."*

It is not enough to just "not think" of negative thoughts and the bad alternatives regarding what we are believing. It can be infuriating to get advice from people who say, "O, just don't worry about it," because it is not that simple. Even though this advice is well meaning, people should say, "Don't worry about it, but instead think about pure, lovely and good things when that thought comes to mind." Then while we are waiting on manifestation to come we can be like children who stay awake at night with excitement wondering what they got for their birthdays and how their parents will surprise them. Remember Jesus loves the faith of children.

Due Season

REMEMBER, BEFORE WE START asking when God's promises and his answers to our prayers will manifest, we always have to be cognizant of the fact that they have already been completed. Realizing that God has already provided for us is a fundamental concept we must hold while waiting on manifestation. When we know our requests are already handled, the anxiety of waiting for our due season is over. Why? Simple, when people have checks coming from jobs, they know the money will come because the process has already been finished. The work has been completed, and the employers' payments have been submitted, as well. All we have to do is wait for the money to show during its "due season," which is our payday. Remember in 2 Peter 1:3 when Scripture talks about all things pertaining to life and godliness that have been done. As long as our desires pertain to life, and a godly life, then we know those desires will manifest in their due season, because they are already ours. With that fact understood, we now need to examine the laws of manifestation. The concrete laws of the earth, both physical and spiritual, govern our world, such as the law of gravity: *"What goes up must come down"* or Newton's First Law of Motion: *"An object at rest stays at rest, and an object in motion stays in motion with the same speed and in the same direction, unless acted upon by an unbalanced force."* These are physical concrete laws that have been tested to be true time after time. The concrete laws in the spiritual realm, like the laws of seed, time and harvest, have been proven, too.

Amazingly, these spiritual laws are evidenced in the physical realm, also. We know that if a person takes a plant seed, puts it in the ground during the right soil temperature and gives it water and sunlight, that seed will grow and sprout into its plant. The same is true for our faith seeds that I mentioned earlier; we all question God's timing. *"Lord, if I do all that I am supposed to concerning this thing, when will it happen . . . when will it manifest?"* Even with this fair question, that we all have asked in prayer at some point, we must remember the law associated with seed, *time* and harvest. The *time* portion of this law is our *waiting season*, which I covered already, while the harvest portion is called our *due season*. *"So when is the due season?"* The word *"due"* as used in Galatians 6:9, also means "proper," so when is the *proper* time? Recognizing the proper time depends on several factors; however, here are some realizations I learned when praying:

- First, we can ask the Lord to reveal the proper time.
- Second, we can stand in faith and claim the proper time with the authority Jesus gave us.
- Finally, we can understand and trust the Lord that he knows the proper time, according to Ecclesiastes 3:1–8, Habakkuk 2:3 and Isaiah 55:11 AMP.

Another great lesson I learned about expecting from God is that *"everything under the sun has a season,"* just like Ecclesiastes states. I disagree with the *"you can have whatever you want when you want"* teaching that seems to be trending today. I have lived through the Bible's truth of how we move from prayer to manifestation; I have literally watched the truth unfold like a guidebook in front of my eyes.

Now please listen to what I mean by saying I disagree with the *"you can have whatever you want when you want"* teaching. I grew up in a *"word of faith"* church and whole-heartedly believe there is biblical Truth to speaking over our seed and claiming what we are expecting, but the Scriptures pertaining to our words and our manifestation has to be "rightly divided" like Timothy 2:15

says. Some popular teachers use this biblical presumption to the wrong end by trying to turn the God of heaven into a magic genie or a cosmic vending machine where all we need to do is push E6 on his keypad to get our prayers answered, just like pushing E6 to get the candy bar from the machine in the office break room. I cannot stress this enough, I am not disagreeing with the biblical truths about the power and the ability our words have, because they are meant to represent a mountain-moving faith.

I will never forget one of the most sobering thoughts God told me during this time in my life, particularly when I got to this topic. He said, *"Son, you would not believe how many people are in hell right now because of this falsehood."* I said, *"Lord, what do you mean?"* He answered, *"They are not in hell because they believed this false teaching about having whatever they want from me and when they want it, because that's not what damns a person to Hell, rejection of my son Jesus condemns. However, the enemy uses this false teaching as a wedge to get in, and once what they were expecting to show didn't manifest, the enemy used that disappointment and anger to turn them completely away from me by making them believe that I was a lie. Some said in their hearts, 'Well if God lied about this, then the Bible can't be the absolute truth, and the Gospel isn't the absolute truth.' Some were people who once followed me."*

This broke my heart when I heard him because it is true. Think about how many times we have heard someone talk as if God does not answer prayer or seen in movies that prayer is a last-ditch effort that portrays God as a magic genie in heaven "deciding" if he will answer or not. This is simply not true, my friends; the God of Abraham, Isaac and Jacob, the God of heaven is a good Father, and the Bible says his promises are "*Yes* and *Amen!*" However, we must apply his Word correctly and faithfully to every situation.

While waiting for manifestation, do not be fooled into thinking the enemy won't attack. The Devil knows that if we believers get our breakthroughs, then others will see and ask how it happened. Once that testimony comes out, and people hear about the goodness of God, then it will cause them to look into the Truth, which ultimately will lead to them hearing the Gospel message at some point. Everything the enemy uses to attack us has a root in something else. The *"what if"* that I outlined in an earlier chapter is no different. Its genesis is fear; in order to defeat this fear, we must take the time to ask ourselves, *"What are we afraid of?"* For me, the answer to this question was two-fold.

1. *What if the thing I'm expecting does not come at all?*
2. *What if the thing I'm expecting does not come in time?*

Within these first questions, I have found four different concepts that must be understood: God Is Against Unanswered Prayer; God Will Sustain; Not Yet; and The Underlying Need.

God Is Against Unanswered Prayer:

Back in the *Our Request, His Will* chapter, I hinted towards the fact God is against unanswered prayer. To prove this point I want to share the wisdom the Holy Spirit gave me. This is why we can be absolutely confident that when we are expecting from God, the answer will manifest, regardless of what the world thinks. I know because God is against unanswered prayers. Like most parents, we would not encourage our kids to do anything that we would not do ourselves. One day the Holy Spirit asked me, *"If God is against you doing something, then why would he do it* himself?" Then he guided me to James 2:15-16 AMP where the Bible says, *"Suppose you see a brother or sister who has no food or clothing, and you say, 'Goodbye and have a good day; stay warm and eat well'—but then you don't give that person any food or clothing. What good does that do?"* When I read that, it hit me like a train when I understood what the Lord was saying. When we doubt, at the root of that doubt, we are saying, *"What if this thing doesn't happen? What if my needs aren't met?"* If we are walking in real expectant faith, then we can be sure something is going to manifest. God promises that he is against us not providing for others what they need, so if he is against that action, then he will not do it. Look at the Scripture again, *"Suppose you see a brother or sister who has no food or clothing, and you* say, *'Good-bye and have a good day; stay warm and eat well'*—but then you don't give that person any food or clothing." The end of this verse indicates that we have the means to do something to help that person. If God is telling us it's wrong if we do not help someone, when we can, then why would he not respond? Why would God, Creator of heaven and earth, who has all the means in the universe to help, not answer our prayers? Lastly, God promised us in Isaiah 55:11 that his Word will not return void or without effect. This is another irrefutable sign that the Lord is against unanswered prayers because he is against void words.

God Will Sustain:

Now that this point is understood, there is a word that we must understand in going forward; the word is "sustain," which means *"to strengthen or support physically or mentally."* When writing the notes for this chapter, this word kept coming up over and over again. Then the Lord showed me that he will always sustain us, even while we are waiting. Psalm 55:22 AMP says, *"Cast your cares on the LORD, and he will sustain you; he will never let the righteous be shaken."* Even when we go through a waiting period, it is vital that we know God will keep us until our manifestation comes. This builds ultimate trust in God, and faith that renders the fear inert. When the fear that sparks the question, *"What if it doesn't happen?"* comes, we have to remember the promise of God when he said in Galatians 6:7–9 AMP,

> Do not be deceived, God is not mocked [he will not allow himself *to be ridiculed, nor treated with contempt nor allow* his *precepts to be scornfully set aside]; for whatever a man sows, this and this only is what he will reap. For the one who sows to his flesh [his sinful capacity, his worldliness, his disgraceful impulses] will reap from the flesh ruin and destruction, but the one who sows to the Spirit will from the Spirit reap eternal life. Let us not grow weary or become discouraged in doing well, for at the proper time we will reap, if we do not give in.*

Rest in faith that God will sustain us, just like he sustained Elijah in 1 Kings 17:15.

Not Yet:

Another key idea to understand is the "not yet" concept. I mentioned that the Bible says in 1 Peter that all things that have to do with a godly life have been done. Even though this is very true, we must understand that just because God has answered already, it doesn't mean those answers will manifest on our timetable. There are some requests that we ask from God that he may have every intention of fulfilling, but it's his will for us to not have it yet; and no matter how much faith we have, it cannot trump his will. For example, I have two beautiful daughters, my oldest Brileigh and my baby Carlynn. Their mother and I want them to experience biblical, romantic love and all that it entails. From the butterflies that come when they first hold a boy's hand, all the way until they get married and have physical intimacy for the first time. All these things are good and designed to be holy gifts from God. But, we definitely don't want them to have that until the right time in their lives. And at ages seven and five . . . the right time is a long time in the future, to say the least. The same principle goes in our lives. Many of us may have been asking God for something for many years now. We have been faithful, persistent, and diligent concerning this request, but we may think the answer still has not come. Before getting discouraged and losing faith, remember it just may not be time yet, or it may not be something he wants for us, period. If it's the former situation, remember that God's will and his plans toward us are always to bless and never hurt. And if it's just not the right time yet, know and trust he will sustain us until it is time. So ultimately the reason we don't have to worry, if we face a "not yet" from the Lord, is because we have ironclad promises in the Bible that speak to his provision, healing, peace and our other needs. Also, we have unbreakable promises that God will keep his Word. Habakkuk 2:3 AMP says, *"For the revelation awaits an appointed time; it speaks of the end and will not prove false. Though it linger, wait for it; it will certainly come and will not delay."*

We reach a whole new level of spiritual maturity when we stop and ask God, "Lord, what do You want in this situation?" When we do this, we are showing everyone that we are putting all our faith and trust in his hands. That's the kind of faith the Roman centurion in Matthew had that made Jesus well pleased!

The Underlying Need:

The last point in this area I want to target is when God answers "*No.*" Not many people talk about this because we don't like to be told "No." In our world of "instant access" and "immediate approval," we have developed a culture of "Yes, yes yes!" But what do we do when the Lord says "*No?*" We do have options: we can pursue our wants and make them happen with our own efforts aside from the blessing of God; and we see how that worked out for Abraham and Sarah when they wanted a son and didn't wait on God; or we can trust that God will supply our underlying needs . . . "*What do you mean?*" The Lord said in Jeremiah 1:5 AMP, *"Before I formed you in the womb I knew you, before you were born, I set you apart; I appointed you as a prophet to the nations."* God knew each of us before we were even thought of being born. This means that he knows our needs, wants, desires and everything in between. Not only that, but he knows what we actually need, too. While going through this season of my life, the Lord showed me this angle I had never seen before then.

Looking at this concept through the lens of being a parent, I see my girls become whiny and insufferable when they do not get the candy they want. It never fails to happen right after a good meal: they will say that they are hungry, or hot or bored, while crying and complaining. Any person who has watched kids before will know, they do not need any of the things they are demanding; instead, they need a nap. The nap is their underlying need, and being the adults in the situation, we know not to give them the candy or toy, but to give our little loved ones what they truly need, which is a comfortable place to lie down and sleep. It's the same way we act toward our Heavenly Father. We may be asking God for more money, but he may not give us the physical cash we think we need, because what we really need is the knowledge and wisdom to do better with what we have. In cases like this, it's best to remember Scriptures like Isaiah 55:11 AMP, when the Lord says that his Word [promises] accomplishes what HE wants. In some instances, we may plan to use his Word to accomplish Y in our lives, but he wants it to accomplish Z. But don't fret, his Z is much better than our Y! The Amplified Bible in Hebrews 13:5 states, *"He will not, he will not, he will not let you down."*

Finally, no matter the situation or concept we see, we must avoid falling into the mental trap that I fell into before God's revelation. Remember I shared that I had adopted the attitude that, "I'm not going to pursue until I know it's God's will"; and then he answered me, *"Unless you pursue . . . you won't ever find out if it was my will."* The sobering truth is that we will never see God sustain us or see our underlying needs met, if we are not in faith, actively pursuing him and his promises.

The second question I asked God was, "What if my answer does not come in time?" I literally said, "Lord, what happens when I have a need, but the manifestation isn't "due" by the time I need or desire it?" He answered, *"First come to the realization that I am not slow or late in fulfilling my promises,"* according to 2 Peter 3:8–9 AMP. Some translations even go as far as saying that he does not *"drag* his *feet."* This does not only pertain to our prayer requests, but also to all his promises. Then the Lord said, *"Second, you must understand the fact that your construct of time is nothing to me."* This is true because remember the Bible says that to God *"a day is a thousand years,"* so our concept of time is useless to him. I admit this is a hard pill to swallow but hear me out. One of the cool things about Jesus living among us is that he stepped from eternity into "our" time. He experienced our issues and restrictions, including human time, so he understands. Therefore, God is not dumb; he knows when we truly need something. Earlier I gave the analogy of a man sitting on a boat watching another man in the water drowning and crying out for help. I used this picture to drive home the fact that God will not give us something useless; in the same sense, the man in the boat would not give the drowning person an ice cream cone over a flotation device. Continuing with that line of thought, God will also not give us what we need after the time we need it. What sense would it make for the man on the boat to throw a flotation device out to the drowning man *after* he had already drowned and died?

So I believe that in regard to time sensitive issues, we can expect absolute guarantees that God's anticipated manifestations will come by the time we need and desire them, if we remain in complete faith for those requests.

My Old Way of Thinking: "Devil's Deception"

Manifest of God's promises will come in "due season." Since the due season could come after the time it's needed, then there is no sense to expect it by the time I need or desire it. There is no 100 percent guarantee that I will get it by that time.

*Before my learning, I would completely stop believing for anything if what I asked for didn't come immediately, with me thinking everything was lost.

My New Way of Thinking: "With Biblical Backing"

Manifestations do come in "due season"; however, *God promised that something will come because* his *Word isn't void, Isaiah 55:11, and what he promises, he does, Numbers 23:19.*

Scriptures . . .

- He will still supply our underlying need because doing so agrees with his will–*Phil* 4:19; 1 *John* 5:14
- Our faith is more precious than gold, he will *not* discard it–1 *Peter* 1:7

- Regardless, God promised his manifestation will not be late–*Hab* 2:3
- God is not slow to fulfill his promise–2 *Peter* 3:9
- His words will not return to him void or without effect–*Isaiah* 55:11
- God is not a liar and what he promises, he does–*Num* 23:19
- Nor will he let you down–*Heb* 13:5 *AMP*
- Nor will he forsake you–*Deut* 31:6
- Nor will he give you less or worse than what you asked for–*Matthew* 7:11

We must all understand that God has his own timetable. I will be the first to admit that this idea drove me absolutely crazy. It seemed like a giant catch all of emotions when expecting the Lord to answer. While waiting for my breakthrough, I had well-meaning friends and family call me and say, "Well, it's in God's timing." It literally made me cringe like a kid who constantly gets told, "When we get ready," after asking his parents when he can open his Christmas gifts. But the most frustrating idea for me wasn't that God's promise seemed vague in my questioning "*When will this happen?*" but the thought that the manifestation truly was in God's timing, not mine. Through all the waiting, we must trust the Lord and maintain the same posture as that of the writer in Psalm 31:15 AMP, when David said to the Lord, "*My times are in your hands.*"

Hindrances

IN LIFE THERE ARE many reasons that something could go wrong with our plans. For example, a golfer can start to make a perfect golf swing but at the last second make a move that will destroy his shot. Such is true in our faith life, too. We can sow the right seeds, stand in faith, and believe God, but after all that, the unexpected can hinder or even altogether kill our harvest. However, before we dig deeper into this idea, it is important to get a good handle on what "hindrance" really means. The word can also mean "frustrated" or "cut off." The Bible says that from the moment Daniel first prayed to God, an angel was dispatched to bring him manifestation. However, the angel was "*hindered.*" Therefore, it's important to remember our prayers may have very well already been answered, but were "held up, frustrated and cut off" for one reason or another. In this chapter, I share an itemized list to show areas that I have found through Scripture and personal experience that can be hindrances. While reading through the list and the explanation, pray that the Holy Spirit reveals those that apply to you. At the very least, I pray you can learn from my experiences of what you should not do, while waiting for manifestation, so my failures can be your triumphs.

Potential Hindrances

1. Doubt and Fear

2. Sin aka "Rebellion"
3. Treatment of Spouse and Others
4. Unforgiveness
5. People
6. Wrong Motives
7. Listening to the Wrong Answer

Doubt and Fear:

Many people know the song, *The Sound of Silence* by Simon & Garfunkel. The song starts off with the lyrics, "Hello darkness my old friend..." [1] Personally, those lyrics come to my mind every time I am tempted with doubt and fear. These two thoughts have relentlessly attacked me my whole life, but the only difference from the song lyrics is that neither doubt nor fear is anyone's "friend." Remember doubt comes in many forms and many names. The Bible speaks of one of these names as having a "double mind" in James 1:5–8. When doubt and fear come, we have to ask ourselves, "*What is causing the doubt in my mind?*" Then much like a sore muscle, we may have to dig deep to hit the exact spot that is causing the pain. I have mentioned before that I played basketball most of my life, and I will never forget when I was hitting my growth spurt around age sixteen. My knees would cause mind numbing pain. It was always my patella tendon, and the doctor told me that it was just the pounding of my activities mixed with natural growth that caused the pain. My mother would rub out the pain when I asked, and I remember she would have to dig around to hit the exact spot that caused the issue. Boy, I am here to tell you when she did find that spot, a zing of pain would shoot up my leg and explode in my mind. I use this example to show that just like digging into the sore spot on a muscle, we must dig in to find the "sore spot" in our faith that is causing fear, doubt, and double mind. Once we find

---

1. Simon and Garfunkel, *Sound of Silence*, lines 1–2.

Hindrances

the source of our doubt, then we must fight it with what God says about the topic at hand. After that, follow the process: rinse, lather and repeat every time the fear arises again.

Earlier I shared how the Lord issued a warning to remind me that the sin that once held me captive before I became a Christian will relentlessly pursue me to try and get me back in its captivity. I have learned through the years that this is true for fear and doubt, as well. I am sure that many reading this book can relate, and like me, look back on their respective lives and see that fear and doubt has stolen so much by taking countless amounts of peace and joy. Perhaps fear still stalks you; doubt still calls your name. And just like the Komodo dragon lizard that bites its prey, and then patiently sits back and watches as the bacteria from the bite slowly weakens and destroys, fear and doubt have done the same to me and you. I have amazing news for you, child of the Most High, just because the enemy will try does not mean he will succeed. To quench fear's assault on our lives, we must do two things. First, we have to do what I call "expect the punch," meaning we have to be in anticipation of the enemy's attack, daily. Second, we have to fight the "fight of faith." I will go more in depth in the *Real Faith* chapter; however, I want to remind you now that faith and fear are relatives, and the only way to kill one is to grow the other.

One other thing that I have learned from the Lord is that I had the wrong kind of thinking regarding "toughness." Somewhere along the way, I adopted the thought, *"You should be tougher than that."* It may have come from my sports background with coaches screaming for years, *"You have to be mentally tough, son!"* But somehow, I believed that I should be able to withstand being around negativity and others who doubt, while waiting for my manifestation. However, this is not true. Look at the story of Jesus raising a little girl from the dead in Matthew 9:23–26:

> *When Jesus entered the synagogue leader's house and saw the noisy crowd and people playing pipes, he said, 'Go away. The girl is not dead but asleep.' But they laughed at him. After the crowd had been put outside, he went in*

and took the girl by the hand, and she got up. News of this spread through all that region.

Look at this story closely. The Bible says, " . . . *but they laughed . . .* " when Jesus said that the little girl was not dead. That gives us a clear indication that they doubted. As a result, Jesus ordered them out, and he removed all doubt from the situation, so faith, especially faith that strong, had no opposition present. I have learned that we need to follow the Lord's lead and remove all doubt from our situations. This may include friends, family and maybe even spouses. I am not talking about removing them from our lives as in shunning, divorce, or other extreme measures, but I am advocating that there are times that we should not share with others what we are believing and waiting for from God. The enemy can easily use other people, with their knowledge or not, to sabotage our faith and hinder our results. I mean look at what happened to Joseph when he told his brothers about what was on his heart from the Lord, yikes. Furthermore, the Bible offers a warning at the end of James 1:5–8 to anyone who doubts:

> *If any of you lacks wisdom, you should ask God, who gives generously to all without finding fault, and it will be given to you. But when you ask, you must believe and not doubt, because the one who doubts is like a wave of the sea, blown and tossed by the wind. That person should not expect to receive anything from the Lord. Such a person is double-minded and unstable in all they do.*

Although the writer is talking about wisdom in the Scripture, he makes a point to say that if we doubt God here, then don't expect anything from him. Doubt is a cancer that, if left untreated, will spread throughout the body of faith and kill it. The only way to kill doubt is to fight it with faith. Faith comes only by hearing the Word of God, so I encourage us to dive into the Word and see what God has to say about our requests. Then adopt the mindset that "*even if the thing I am pursuing doesn't come, it must be because it does not line up with God's plan of peace for me in my life. I trust him completely, so what he wants is what I want.*" This kind of thinking only comes when we remember that his will is always good towards us, always.

If we want to see a great example of doubt and how it can lead to a delay of our manifestations, we need look no further than the children of Israel and their exodus from Egypt. They experienced possibly the most impressive story of hindered manifestation of all time. Their trip was only supposed to take about a week or two, but their journey lasted forty years. In the book of Exodus, God told Moses that he was going to bring his children out of the slavery and bondage that they were under at the hands of Pharaoh. God told the Israelites that he had prepared a land *"flowing with milk and honey,"* and all they had to do was trust him. As we read the story, we find that the people committed various sins against the Lord, but one in particular caused the hindrance of the manifestation of reaching the promised land, and for some people, it canceled their arrival altogether.

In the book of Numbers, the Bible speaks in detail about twelve Israelite spies who were sent to scout the land that God had promised them. When we read the story, we see that eleven of the twelve men came back with what the Bible calls, *"evil report."* As we continue to read chapters 13-14, we find the eleven spies came back and talked about how *"low and outmanned"* the Israelites were compared to the inhabitants of the land. The spies said that they were *"grasshoppers"* compared to the natives, and basically, had no prayer of winning and taking that land from the giants already living there. As a result of their view, Numbers 14:1-4 says,

> *And all the children of Israel murmured against Moses and against Aaron; and the whole congregation said unto them, 'Would God that we had died in the land of Egypt! Or would God we had died in this wilderness! And why hath the Lord brought us unto this land to fall by the sword, that our wives and our children should be a prey? Were it not better for us to return into Egypt?' And they said one to another, 'Let us make a captain, and let us return into Egypt.'*

The Bible called what the spies said an *"evil report"* for two reasons. First, it was directly against what God promised he would do. God said "Yes," but they said, "No." The eleven spies were moved by what they saw, instead of standing unwavering in what God said. Second, this caused the nation of Israel to doubt the Lord and rebel against Moses, when they heard the spies' report. We find that because of what these eleven men said, God swore that an entire generation would not see the Promised Land because they allowed the doubt from the elven spies' report to contaminate their faith. There was only one, Caleb the twelfth spy, who said they could have the land because God promised it. Caleb trusted God fully, regardless of what he saw, and as a result, he got to see the Promised Land and much more!

Sin aka "Rebellion:"

Sin aka "rebellion" is another reason that our prayers are hindered at times, which is not the easiest pill to swallow. In the "cancel culture" we live in today; many are afraid to speak against unrighteousness and sin because of the persecution that comes with unpopular ideas. People are afraid that if they speak up, they will lose family, friends, congregations and even careers. However, this should not be an excuse to avoid speaking the truth. God commands us to live holy, not happy. Real Godly happiness is a byproduct of living a holy life before him. It's important to remember that " ... *whom the Lord loveth he chasteneth*," (Hebrews 12:6 KJV). The word *"chasteneth"* is just a fancy way to say "correct." When God corrects us by his word and through his people, it's because he loves us.

Sin is simply rebellion. It's us doing our own thing apart from God's will. The problem with sin is that it is a separating agent. Mankind's sin separated us from God. God in his grace and mercy chose to adopt us and create a way to come back into relationship with him. This way that he created his son Jesus Christ. Through Jesus' death, burial and resurrection, he once and for all time and for all people dealt with the sin issue. However, I think it's a disservice to God's lovingkindness and Jesus' ultimate sacrifice to only look at what the Lord did from a salvation point of view. Even though that is the most important, the "cake" if you will, keep in mind that when Jesus said, *"It is finished"* on the cross, he wasn't only talking about the way to our salvation was finished, but also the way to an abundant life. Sin keeps us from this abundant life.

The Bible says in Isaiah 59:1–2 KJV, *"Behold, the Lord's hand is not shortened, that it cannot save; neither his ear heavy that it cannot hear: But your iniquities have separated between you and your God, and your sins have hid his face from you, that he will not hear."* The abundant life we all seek and want only comes from God the Father, but our sin makes him hide his face and not hear us. It is easy to see how unchecked sin would hinder and altogether stop manifestations to prayer in our lives. Psalm 66:18 AMP states plainly and strongly, *"If I regard sin and baseness in my heart [that is, if I know it is there and do nothing about it], the Lord will not hear [me]."* Sin must be dealt with, and the only way to deal with sin is to confess it to the Lord, repent (change our thinking) and ask his help to overcome it. This sounds simple, but it involves a minute by minute, day by day, year by year process.

Treatment of Spouse and Others:

How we treat others can also hinder our prayer life. The Bible says that everything we do is a seed, and we reap what we sow. If we sow negative words and actions into others' lives, should we expect anything different in our own? Furthermore, to all the men reading this book. If you are a married man, God specifically addresses and draws a parallel between the treatment of your wife and the answers to our prayers. The NLT version of 1 Peter 3:7 says, *"In the same way, you husbands must give honor to your wives. Treat your wife with understanding as you live together. She may be weaker than you are, but she is your equal partner in God's gift of new life. Treat her as you should so your prayers will not be hindered."* Also, to all the married ladies reading this, don't think you have a free pass here. The Bible addresses how you are to honor your husbands and submit to his leadership. Now this is not a marriage book in the least, and I am not going down that trail, but I strongly encourage us all to study the relationship of godly marriages. Marriage, at the end of the day, is a covenant, and if we have not noticed yet, God puts importance on covenants.

This is true for how we treat each other. From the stranger we meet for the first time on a bus to the best friend we have known since we were six years old. Remember that Jesus said in the book of Mark that the greatest command was to love our neighbor and to love God with our all. It's important to note that we cannot have a mentality to "love" our neighbor just to have our prayers answered. That is not love. It's a *quid pro quo* with God, and we always have to remember that he is a King and not a rewards program. We must love for love's sake to be present, to help and to bless each other. No matter the personal background, skin tone, economic status, history, or any other defining characteristics we all have, we must love as God loves us. John 15:13 says, *"Greater love has no more than this: to lay down one's life for one's friends."* Personally, I believe this scripture is not just talking about physically dying for a friend, rather alludes to laying down different areas of our lives for someone else. Maybe we have a full day of fun planned with our family, when a buddy, who is going through a divorce, calls and is so sad that depression is knocking on his door. *Laying down* our lives in this instance would be canceling our plans to just go sit with our friend and love on them. Or if we wanted to lay in bed all day and binge watch a Netflix show on a snowy day but our friend across town needs a ride to the store because their car has broken down. *Laying down* our lives here would be getting out of that warm bed, putting snow boots and a heavy coat on to go help them. I know these are not ground breaking concepts, I am just trying to share different ways to view John 15:13.

Unforgiveness:

When we harbor unforgiveness in our hearts toward others, we are also harboring sin. This goes a bit deeper into an earlier point.

There is no direct Scripture that says word for word, *"If you don't forgive, your prayers will be hindered,"* however unforgiveness is a slippery slope that will ultimately lead to this. Mark 11:25–26 in the New Living Translation says, *"But when you are praying, first forgive anyone you are holding a grudge against, so that your Father in heaven will forgive your sins, too. But if you do not forgive, neither will your Father in heaven forgive your trespasses."* Unforgiveness could be a slippery slope, because remember, the Bible talks about how our sin separates us from God, and if our sins are not forgiven due to unforgiveness towards others like Mark 11:26 says, then sin is still present. And if unrepentant sin is still present in our lives, Isaiah 59: 1–2 and Psalm 66:18 are relevant, and those Scriptures show this sin will ultimately lead to our prayers being hindered because the Lord isn't hearing our prayers.

People:

Sometimes we can do all the right things by Scripture's standards, and our prayers can still be hindered. Before I'm labeled as a heretic, who is claiming that God is a liar, please hear me. Earlier I talked about how God showed me that our promises come from the spirit, through the soul and to the body? The point I am making here is that the "sore spots of our faith" live in the "body" part of this equation. *"The only perfect person is gone now, so God has us to work with,"* while maybe said jokingly, this saying is often used to point out that we humans seem to muck up God's plans sometimes and delay what he wants to happen. But the truth is we can trust that God knows all, even the hindrances, and we can trust him.

This is also true in our lives when God is trying to get something to us. For example, look at Luke 6:38 KJV, *"Give, and it shall be given unto you; good measure, pressed down, and shaken together, and running over, shall men give into your bosom. For with the same measure that ye mete withal it shall be measured to you again."* Inside this promise, the blueprint of *how* our manifestations come is shown. It says, *"Shall men give . . . "* Humans are used by God to bring things into our lives simply because people are in our physical realm. Therein lies a problem. Remember we humans are sinful apart from the blood of Jesus; our every thought is evil. So there is a possibility that our manifestations are hindered because the people to be used are holding it up for some reason that only God knows. They could be doing this out of sheer ignorance or malice. For example, look at slavery in America. President Lincoln decreed that slavery was abolished on January 1, 1863, nationally. However, the decree was not recognized in Texas until June 19, 1863, a whole five months longer before slaves in Texas saw the answer to years of prayer. We will never know why it was delayed by men, but our God knows.

The good news is that though men might seem to slow the manifestations to our prayers, they cannot stop them. All the promises of manifestation from God are centered on our faith and not human will. Being an African American man, I have heard all my life about how I am disadvantaged because I am black, and how the "white man" will keep me down and never let me ascend higher than he. This rhetoric has recently been pushed harder through the media and certain groups. Then I read Scriptures like Isaiah 54:17 which says, *"No weapon formed against you shall prosper, every tongue that rises against you, you (God) shall condemn,"* and James 1:17, *"Every good and perfect gift is from above, coming down from the Father of the heavenly lights, who does not change like shifting shadows."* I grew an understanding of faith and the heart of God towards me, and now I am here to tell everyone who it is that hates us or is jealous of us. No matter our color or background, *the only* person who can stop what God has for you is *you*! In the Scriptures and the promises of God it holds, there are no stipulations of ethnicity, country of origin or economic situation. The only thing that's required is our faith. Faith in who Jesus is and faith God will answer.

That's the premise and title of this book, to have a faith hound mentality. A hound does not care if someone else says he can't have a bone, he only listens to his master. If the master said he can have the bone, then it's his. I adopted the philosophy a long time ago that I am not, and will not, be oppressed by any man, regardless of the color of my skin. If someone does try to oppress me and keep me from God's will for me, then woe to him. If the thing is something God has for me, then they are not fighting me, they are fighting the Lord, and he remains undefeated.

Not Asking or Having Wrong Motives:

Another reason our manifestation could be hindered is because we don't ask, or we ask as the Bible says, "amiss." The Bible makes this clear when it says in James 4:2-3 KJV, *"You lust and do not have. You murder and covet and cannot obtain. You fight and war. Yet you do not have because you do not ask. You ask and do not receive, because you ask amiss, that you may spend it on your pleasures."* The word *amiss* could also mean *improperly*. Remember when I spoke about the sovereignty of God? This sovereignty he has is also the criteria for which he grades our hearts behind our requests. Think of a person who wants a job that pays more money to buy a new home. This seems fine on the surface, but what if in their heart of hearts, the person only wants the house so they can be haughty towards others. Even though the request seems sincere, the heart behind it is "amiss" or improper and wrong. I encourage us to do inventory on all our "pending" prayers and make sure our hearts have the right attitude behind them.

Listening to the Wrong Answer:

Using imagination for a second, picture a man named Tim standing in front of two other men, Man A and Man B. Don't get hung up on the order of the men's names because Man B has priority over Man A. This is a known fact to all parties involved in this scenario. Imagine Tim has been asking for a certain thing to happen but Man A says "No, absolutely not!" Tim goes away dejected and sad thinking that since Man A said, "No," then Man B also said, "No." However, Tim never approached Man B to ask if the answer

Faith Hounds

really was "No." Unbeknownst to Tim, Man A and Man B are at odds with each other. In fact, Man A is actually submissive to Man B, and no matter what Man A says, Man B's word is king. With all this information, what would we say to Tim? Would we tell him to keep pursuing the request and get more information? Of course, we would be right! Now imagine Tim in this story is you, while Man A represents the world, our physical day to day life. Man B represents Almighty God and all his promises.

I touched on this idea earlier in the book. The world's "No" answer does not always equal a "No" response from God. I found that like Tim in this story, I would stop pursuing things I asked God for in prayer because the world said, "No," first. Remember the concept of "faith vs. facts." Yes, facts are important, but they do not always line up with our faith. The Bible is filled with examples of when facts of the world did not match the faith in God, but he did a miracle anyway. I imagine that when we look back on our own lives, there were times when a blessing came, and it made no factual sense, but God did it for us, regardless. If we stop at the first "No" we get without asking God if it came from him, we may miss out on our manifestations. I truly believe that if God does say, "No," it will be accompanied with peace and a redirection of our faith. However, if the answer we have is a "No," then we won't know for sure if the answer was from God or the world until we press in and pursue God.

Previously I wrote about our expectations, and how inside of our expectations lives the work we must do to show our faith. Now I want to share about the "base" of our expectations when they face contradictory reports. When expecting manifestation, we must check the "base" of our expectation. If we are expecting based on physical signs, human's word and other worldly signs, then we have taken faith in God and placed it elsewhere. It is sometimes very easy to get thoughts mixed up when we think that we are placing faith in God and his Word, but we are actually expecting based on what information we are receiving through physical senses. Proof of where our expectation is based is how we react when contradictory information comes that is different from what we are expecting. For example, while I was waiting on my call to start the job I had been wanting, I would hear contradictory information about my start date from the world's point of view, and I would get down and depressed. I was the man the Bible referred to in James when it said, *"For he that wavered is like a wave of the sea driven with the wind and tossed."* If our faith and expectation is based in the Lord, regardless of what information comes from the world, there will be peace, just like Jesus said in John 10:10 and Matt 7:24–27. If we want to see where our expectation and base of faith is, we must check our reactions when information adverse to our faith shows. Remember when contradictory information comes . . . *only believe*. When the world says "No," but we believe God said "Yes" . . . *only believe and pursue!* "Always expect but know the harvest will come when it's due."

Please understand that this is not a conclusive list of hindrances to our prayers. These are just some of the reasons I have experienced firsthand. I wonder which of these possible pitfalls each of you may have encountered. Perhaps it may be fear and doubt that creep in on our prayers, or perhaps we may be harboring unforgiveness or unrepentant sin in our hearts. Maybe none of these, but we are asking from God with the wrong motives, or maybe we have mistreated others. Whatever the hindrance is, the good news is that we have a forgiving Father in heaven whose ear is always ready to hear us and forgive our sin, and then show us where we are disconnected. I encourage us all to bring any hindrance to the throne room of God, lay it at his feet and move forward. Move into the fullness of abundant life that he has for us.

What Comes Instead and Disappointment

My observations and graphics may seem a bit technical for some people, and by no means am I trying to make this God's Word, but I recognize four areas where our manifestations of prayer could fall.

1. *Manifestation isn't due to show in our lives yet (Due Season)*
2. *Manifestation is due but we have to go get it. (Faith Hound)*
3. *Manifestation could be delayed, hindered for some reason (Hindrance)*
4. *What we are expecting doesn't line up with God's Will (Our Request, His Will)*

I have discussed in depth all these areas, however what I will highlight in this chapter has residence in the fourth area: When what we expect does not agree with what God wants.

Imagine a person is expecting a new iPhone. The order is paid; he got the tracking number; and now he is waiting for it to be delivered. Now picture that today is the day it is supposed to show; the confirmation of delivery email from UPS pops up, so he knows it's here. He gets home, picks up the package, takes it inside the house and excitedly rips into the box to find . . . a Samsung Galaxy Note. *What will he do?* At the very least he might be disappointed, because clearly what came is different than what was expected. Now translate that example to our prayer lives. Not many people

What Comes Instead and Disappointment

talk about this aspect, but what do we do when what shows up in our lives is different from what we have been believing God would send? Some "word of faith" teachers seldom admit this feeling or even note it does happen, so what do we do when it does?

First, we must always remember what I discussed in the *Our Request, His Will* chapter. We have to constantly remind ourselves of the sovereignty of God and the message of Isaiah 55:11. This Scripture pushes the fact home that God's Word will not return to him void, and I want to use it to make another point here. The Amplified Bible version of the Scripture reads, *"So will my word be which goes out of my mouth; It will not return to me void (useless, without result), without accomplishing what I desire, And without succeeding in the matter for which I sent it."* God is promising here that his Word will only do what he wants. Therefore, if we are standing on God's Word in expectation for our prayers to be answered, then we need to understand that we must relent to his will and give a wide berth for what he wants to come. If we establish this in our hearts, then no matter what comes, even if it doesn't seem to be what we asked, we will never be disappointed. When we have done all we can and have nothing hindering our requests, then I believe what actually manifests, although possibly being different from expectations, will not be worse or less than what we asked for. Throughout the book, I have shared my faith and experience about how good the Lord is, and how he is the Giver of good gifts by using various Scriptures that break down how good God's will is and how his plans for us are always positive. However, let me give my closing argument in this matter and share what I believe is the 'promise of promises' when it comes to this area of expecting manifestation to prayer.

Perhaps the most interesting thing about Scripture is how one Scripture can speak to a swathe of situations we face in life. Romans 10:11 is one of those Scriptures and says, *"For the Scripture saith, whosoever believeth on him shall not be ashamed."* Primarily, this Scripture is speaking to the salvation of our souls. It's a promise that no matter what we go through in life, as long as our faith is in Jesus, we will not be ashamed. But take a closer look at that word "ashamed," the Greek word *kataischynō* [1], also means *to be disappointed*. As a matter of fact, many other Biblical translations just say "disappointed," instead of "ashamed." *Why does this matter, one may ask?* I believe the New Testament writer is not only saying anyone who puts faith in the Lord will not be disappointed in the afterlife but is also speaking to our present here and now. Isaiah 49:23 also pushes this point deeper when it says,

> Kings shall be your foster Fathers, and their queens your nursing mothers; they shall bow down to you with their faces to the earth and lick up the dust of your feet. Then you will know that I am the LORD, for they shall not be ashamed who wait for me.

Also, there are times when what comes to us is different entirely in substance from what we expect. There are times that we may ask for something physical, but something spiritual, ideological or otherwise may come. We may ask for money, but the Lord might give us a better job to earn more money, or perhaps he may give us the wisdom to invest in a company that is going to be bought out soon, which would give us all the money we might ever need. Our God is an infinite God; therefore, he has infinite possibilities to answer prayer.

Consider my story of how this unfolded in my life. A couple of years ago, I had an old truck I wanted to sell. I had bought this truck from my father-in-law, fixed it up and drove it for a while. At the time, I was just starting to get some of the revelation that I am sharing in this book, so like a new fawn breaking in his legs in the spring, I was excited to take this opportunity to stretch my faith and see what would happened.

I prayed, asking the Lord to help me sell the truck for the amount of money I wanted and all that comes with selling a vehicle. I advertised the sale of the truck on Facebook, Craigslist and other popular sales platforms. I had some tire kickers, but no one would commit. I started getting frustrated, because I was thinking that the truck just would not sell. Then one night, I got an idea, *"Why*

---

1. Popovich, Greek Word Kataischynō

don't you put the truck on the open lot by the church?" You see, there is an old vacant lot by my church where people leave vehicles all the time to sell them. I have passed this area often over most of my life while going to church, and it just slipped my mind. I placed the truck there on that lot, and within one night, I had a bidding war and sold it for more than I had originally asked for that truck. This is a real-world example of what I have been believing. I prayed for the sale of the truck and expected it directly. However, what *came instead* was the idea to place the truck in that lot, which led to the sale for a higher price. If I had given up because of my original disappointment, I would not have received what the Lord really had for me in this situation. Just like when Jesus said, specifically about prayer, in Luke 11:13, *"You Fathers—if your children ask for a fish, do you give them a snake instead? Or if they ask for an egg, do you give them a scorpion? Of course not! So if you sinful people know how to give good gifts to your children, how much more will your heavenly Father give the good gifts to those who ask him?"* This confirms what I stated earlier, "He will not give worse or less than what we asked for." I don't know about you, readers, but getting a snake when I asked for fish, and scorpion when I asked for an egg is way less and way worse.

Real Faith

I HAVE A CONFESSION to make, out of this entire book I have dreaded writing this chapter the most. Dreaded it not in the sense that I just did not want to write it but dreading it like getting out of a warm bed on a cold snowy morning. Dreading to write it, knowing that this chapter is such a big undertaking, and praying I don't miss anything. I have to give this chapter the respect it deserves, because faith is a most powerful topic. Faith is our currency in the spirit realm. Faith's very presence, or lack thereof, in our hearts can cause even Jesus to marvel and be impressed. Don't believe me? Look at the Gospels: two times it was recorded when Jesus had a visceral response to people's faith. Once when he, Jesus, went from village to village performing miracles, and the folks there refused to believe. The Bible said that he "*marveled at their disbelief.*" The other time was with the Roman officer who impressed Jesus by his faith. If that does not convince how important faith is then listen to what the Bible says in Hebrews 11:1, "*Without faith it is impossible to please God.*" We can't even try to please him if we don't have faith first. Our faith also draws out the power of the Lord and lays the groundwork for his intervention in our lives. When we read the story about the woman with the issue of blood, the Bible talks about Jesus knowing power had left him when she touched him. Why would he know, one may ask? Because she touched him with faith. Jesus was essentially in a mob in this story with people touching him left and right. Some of them touched the Lord out of curiosity, anger, fear, and doubt. But this dear woman was the only one who touched him out of faith that he could heal her. That faith activated her blessing and drew the attention of Christ. Simply put, when we touch the Lord with our faith, it draws out his power.

I already shared about the knowledge I received in regard to 1 Peter 1:7. The Lord used this verse to show me that faith will never be disregarded or thrown away; however, it may be redirected at times. But redirected to what? I believe that when faith is redirected by the Lord, it is pointed to whatever God has for us in that situation. Before we grill a steak, we first must own a steak, right? Consequently, if we don't even have the steak in the first place, we have to go get one. Same idea with the issue of faith, for faith to be used or redirected, we must first have faith, and if we don't have faith, we must go get it. The good news is that unlike the steak analogy I used, we already have some faith. The Word of God says at the end of Romans 12:3, *"God has dealt each man a measure of faith."* But just because we have faith does not mean that it's strong or that the faith we do have is in the area we are needing for a miracle. What do we do with this measure of faith; how do we build and where do we go to get faith in a specific area where we may be lacking?

God's Word is the answer! Just as we may go to Walmart, Kroger's, or H.E.B to get that ribeye steak we are craving, we must go to the Bible to get and build our faith for the requests we are believing in God to give us. Romans 10:17 says, *"Faith comes by hearing, and hearing by the word of God."* Simply put, if we need faith or want to build our faith on a certain issue, then we need to *hear* what God says about it. Remember what he said is in his Word, and like previously discussed, I am walking proof that he will lead us to his will in that situation, because he promised he would. I have heard the metaphor with the Bible mentioned as a bag, and all the Scriptures in it are seeds. If people want healing, then they should seek healing seeds in the Bible like Isiah 53:5, or if they need joy in their lives, then they should seek out seeds in the Bible that pertain to joy, such as Psalm 16:11.

Once people see what God has to say about their desires, and they have their seeds of Scripture to prove it . . . how do they show their faith? One may ask, *"Wait, you can show faith?"* The answer is a resounding *"Yes!"* Faith is a muscle that must be worked in order to be productive, or it will grow weak and feeble. The only way to show our faith is by what we say and do in our lives. While Jesus was talking about false prophets and warning his followers about deceivers, he said in Matthew that we will " *. . . know them by their fruit . . .* " meaning that we will know what is in a person's heart by what they do and speak.

When examining the fact that what we do and say shows our faith, we have to appreciate the power of our words. We have already discussed the power of our words, but what about our actions? What we do is just as vital as what we say. The writer in James 2:18 says, *"But someone will say, 'You have faith; I have deeds.' Show me your faith without deeds, and I will show you my faith by my deeds."* Notice how he specifically targets the argument that many of us have heard from people when they claim to have faith, but don't show it. James says I will *show* what I believe *by* what I do. This harkens back to what was mentioned about Jesus' warning about false prophets, *"You will know them by what they do."* This is the number one defense I take when I discuss the *"once saved, always saved"* doctrine that is so popular. True, no one can *take* our salvation, just like my seven-year-old daughter cannot take $100 from my wallet. But we can *give* our salvation away and lose fellowship with the Lord, just like I can *give* her the money. We can give our salvation away by what we do or don't do. If we claim to be believers, but do not actively follow the Lord, can we really say we believe? I mainly use this example to push the importance of our words and works of faith.

The other aspect of faith we need to look at now is our works. Our actions are just as important and telling as our words are, because not only do they show our words, but those actions also validate our words. Think about a man who may be physically abusing his wife. Sure, he may say he loves and cares for her, but his actions tell a much different tale. As mentioned earlier, some people say they are Christians, and they say all the right things, but live sinful unrepentant lifestyles. Jesus said regarding people like this, they "*. . . honor me with their mouths but their hearts are far from me."* There are some simple and general facts we must understand about faith and works.

1. *Faith and works are two separate things.*
   Remember these two are not one and the same. Faith is only shown by what we speak and do.

2. *Faith makes works.*
   When we really have true faith, I have come to learn that it generates good works. When I came to the Lord, I knew a change had taken place because the faith I professed made me want to do things to show it.

3. *Faith without works is fake.*
   The Bible makes this clear as day in the book of James. Without works the faith one claims to have is inactive and dead.

4. *What we do and say only shows faith that is real. Consequently, only real active faith gets the promise in our lives. Rom 4:16*
   Earlier I mentioned that faith is our currency to receive from the Lord, because all answered prayer depends entirely on our faith in God's Word. Our works cannot obtain the promises of God because they are only meant to show our faith that is in our heart, according to (James 2:22).

5. *The test of our faith is to see if we really believe what we say.*
   When faith is put to work on a request, *it will always be tested to see* if it's real.
   This will be covered in depth in another chapter, but our faith must stand trial to see if we really believe what we say. James 1:3 talks about faith being "tried" which means to be proven.

I have played basketball all my life. I remember my college coach used to get on us if we made a little extra move when coming off a screen trying to be "cute," as he put it, instead of driving hard to the basket and scoring. Coach would call this, "wasted energy," and this thinking has stayed with me through the years. I look at things I do and determine if they are a waste of energy instead of getting straight to the point. I have come to learn this thinking has merit in the spiritual realm also. Remember earlier, I shared that God is against unanswered prayers, and I believe he is against wasted energy, too. What does wasted energy look like in the arena of faith and how do we avoid it? While waiting for manifestation to a prayer, we can ask ourselves and the Lord, *"What is the work of faith that I can do that is appropriate in this situation?"* If you are a woman and are believing in God for a husband, what could your work be to show the faith that's in your heart? It could be that you join a Christian adult group or study God's Word to work on issues that would make you a better wife before you meet the man and say I do. Do faithful actions, instead of the wasted energy of going to bars or night clubs and talking to men who you know God does not want for you. Maybe you are a freshman in high school, and your heart's desire is to get a full-ride NCAA Division I football scholarship. The problem might be that you are undersized compared to the average college athlete. Your work of faith will be to train every second you can and hone your craft. While you are doing that, you are pursuing the Kingdom of God by volunteering at your church. The Lord could help you grow six full inches during your junior summer making you a six feet six inches tall, 266 pounds machine, who will have schools fighting over you during your senior year. Work in faith, instead of the wasted energy of not obeying your parents and pursuing other activities that won't get you where you want to be. The point I'm making is that God has made our faith so powerful we can use it like a finely tuned weapon to secure our hearts' desires. The next question might be, *"Ok, how long do I continue to show my faith until it manifests?"* Again, I talked about this in another chapter, but the short answer is, *until manifestation arrives.* Remember Daniel prayed for a long time that God would help him in the midst of the king's decree. Finally, one day an angel showed up and said, *"Do not be afraid, Daniel. Since the first day that you set your mind to gain understanding and*

REAL FAITH

to humble yourself before your God, your words were heard, and I have come in response to them."

If we continue studying the story, the angel explains that Daniel's answer was on its way but got held up or hindered. The point here is that the answer was on its way immediately, and if Daniel had given up, then he *would not have seen his answer manifest*. Like James 2:26 says, *"Just like the body is dead without breath, faith is dead without good work."* Substitute the word *dead* in the Scripture for *inactive*. We must keep working to show the faith that's in our hearts until manifestation shows.

This illustration is a perfect representation of how God wants to blend a beautiful medley of our faith and works in our hearts and lives.

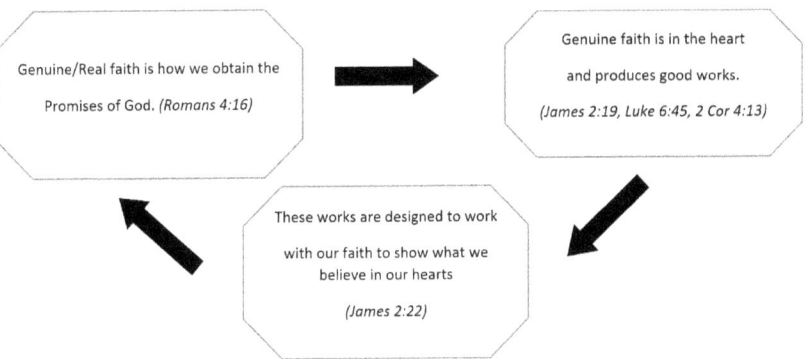

When I created this diagram, it hit me that the ideas all flow into each other, and if one is missing, then the whole system will fall. Starting with the genuine faith in God's promise, this is the only way we obtain the promises of God; however, this genuine faith resides in the heart, and it makes us show what we believe by our actions. These works are only designed to collaborate with the faith that we say we have, which leads us back to the real faith we must have to allow the manifestation in our lives. This is a continual cycle with each step feeding off its predecessor, *while* it feeds its successor.

Faith Hounds

While living in this relationship of faith and works, always remember my friends, the common theme that God is faithful, no matter what, and our faith has only one of two ends with him. Either our requests are answered how we pray them, or they are redirected; they are *never* disregarded! Before moving on, I will issue a warning about falling into another trap, like I did, the trap of waiting. Now this statement may seem counter to my discussion about "waiting," but this time, I am not talking about waiting on God, rather I am talking about us waiting for everything to be "right" before we act. It's a common idea that we hear from others and think ourselves in various arenas of life. Perhaps someone may be waiting to look for a husband until things are "perfect" in their mind. I have news for you, things are never "perfect," and more often than not, conditions are not likely to be ideal to make a move of faith. Ecclesiastes 11:4 in the Amplified Bible version says it perfectly, *"He who watches the wind [waiting for all conditions to be perfect] will not sow [seed], and he who looks at the clouds will not reap [a harvest]."* This verse tells us that real faith does not wait for everything to be ideal. Real faith considers our every circumstance before we sow the seeds of our faith to begin our good works. Remember the Bible says the Kingdom of God suffers violence, and the violent take by force, while also remembering that God won't *redirect* our faith if we are not even using it in the first place. Be a true faith hound, use the weapon of faith, pursue, and take all God has for us by force in Jesus Name! If there is redirection needed, let it come from the Lord alone.

After sharing how I got my position with my current employer, I want to give another clear-cut real-world example of the "redirection" concept in action. While I was waiting to be hired with this company, I started to have many dreams at night. Up to that point, I had always felt that the Lord spoke to me in dreams because that was the time when my mind was quiet, and my body was at rest. I then came across a book by Mark Virkler and Charity Virkler-Kayembe called, *Hearing God Through Your Dreams*.[1] In their book, the authors go into vast detail on the correlation

---

1. Virkler and Virkler-Kayembe, Hearing God, 1–30.

between Scripture and how God speaks to us in our dreams. It's a fantastic read, and I highly recommend it. One portion of the book that really hit home for me was the role play in our dreams. The book proposes that when God uses numbers in our dreams, they are literal, as evidenced in the dreams that Joseph had. Every dream that he had, which included a number, represented that exact number in some form in his real life. For example, Joseph had eleven brothers and had a dream that eleven stars were bowing to him.

One night I had a dream, and in this dream, I remember it was a beautiful day with blue skies and no clouds. I was standing on a sidewalk facing my old middle school. On the right side of me was a fence that was exactly nine feet tall. (Remember how I already mentioned that in the Virkler's book that they believed numbers were very literal and were exact representations? Keep this in mind because it plays a major role regarding the nine-foot fence in my dream.) In my dream, I was next to this fence and on the other side of it was a beautiful field full of rolling hills with green lush grass. On my left side was another field, it looked nice and had what I thought were yellow flowers. As I walked down the sidewalk, I noticed that the "petals" on the flowers in the field on the left started to move, and then they turned into bees. These bees all came towards me, and then started to sting me. The stings did not hurt, but I felt the pressure of the stings. At the end of the dream, I heard a voice say, *"This is Will Mitchell, and we have been expecting his family for a long time."* Then I woke up.

Now there were a multitude of revelations God was making to me in this dream. Ones that are not pertaining to the topic of this book, however after praying about the dream, the Lord reminded me of the Virkler's book, and their understanding of the role numbers play. Also, in their book they talk about symbolism in dream and how what we see in the dream represents something in our "waking life," as they call it. After praying, I knew that the fence represented the barrier that was keeping me from what I wanted, which was my new career represented by the rolling green field in the dream. The barrier that I thought was holding me back from the job was a special qualification I needed from the government to work at this site. I was told this process took roughly *nine* months, and by the time I had the dream I was six months into the nine-month process. I took this as the Lord was letting me know my time was coming, and the wait was almost over. I was so excited, I shared the dream with my wife and felt released to quit my current job because I was sure promotion was on the way. Long story short, the remaining three months came and went making the total nine months for this qualification come and go.

I was upset and told the Lord that I didn't understand, and I had already made the decision to quit my other job with the peace to leave my old position. Money was running dry, and I didn't know what to do. Again, the Lord showed that even in our misunderstanding and missing the mark, he is still gracious and protective. He blessed me to get a job at the detention center. Now remember, I shared that at this job I worked nights and began to write the outline of this book. During those nights at the center, the dam of understanding Who God really is broke in my life, and as a result, this book was conceived. Furthermore, God being amazing like he is put the cherry on top when I finally got the job qualification I needed, and I earned the position I hold now, which is better than the one for which I was originally hired. But here is the kicker to the story, that nine foot fence did in fact represent the barrier keeping me from where I wanted to be and where God wanted me to be. However, it was not nine months from the day my qualification process started, but it was in fact, nine months from when I had the dream. Because nine months to the day of having that dream, according to the dream journal I keep, my qualification came in, and I was cleared to start working on site. To me this is a surreal experience to see God's redirection. Even though I did misunderstand the Lord, and in fact, I got what he was saying wrong, I was still moving in faith. While moving in faith, I pursued what I thought was what the Lord wanted for me by quitting my job and waiting for my qualification process to conclude, since the end of the process was near. In actuality, that's not what he had for me, so he "redirected" that faith to what he wanted, which was a quiet place for me to sit at His feet and learn. I believe the importance during this time was that I was pursuing the Kingdom of God by advancing it internally for myself and externally for others. Not to earn "brownie points" or act like I'm superior in any way, because trust me I am not, I just want to highlight a point that I made earlier in this book. I shared that Jesus promises that if we seek the Kingdom, then everything else will be given to us by default. he cares about every aspect of our lives and will provide an escape, just like he did for me.

I continue to declare that out of that time in my life came countless blessings, a deeper revelation and respect for Jesus being chief among them, while this book follows closely behind it. As long as I live, I will always remember this experience and will continue to share with anyone who will listen about how faithful, loving, patient and amazing our God is because I have experienced it first-hand. I have tasted and seen that the Lord is good.

Now let's talk about the power of our faith. I talked about the power of speaking the Word of God, but what about the actual power of our faith in that Word? There is a reason that Jesus said our faith can "move mountains" in our lives. To me the most impressive aspect of faith isn't its ability to "move mountains," which is quite a feat, but its ability to dictate time. Allow me to explain. I am convinced that our faith can indeed dictate our physical realm of time. In the chapter, "Due Season," I talked about our physical space of time as we know it. I used this to push the point home that God does not operate by our time. Even though he does not operate by our timetable, he understands it because he created the construct. I went into depth about waiting for due seasons for manifestations. The Lord showed me that our faith can dictate our physical realm of time in the sense of making manifestation happen. Now please hear me, it is very important to understand that I am not pushing the *"name whatever you want, claim whatever you want then you will get whatever you want."* gospel. I have made it clear that God is not a magic genie who is at our beck and call. However, there is biblical precedent and some credence to believing that our faith is an element in the timing of manifestation.

The story of Jesus and the fig tree in Mark 11 is one basis of my argument for the point I am making, particularly in verses 12–14.

> The next day as they were leaving Bethany, Jesus was hungry. Seeing in the distance a fig tree in leaf, he went to find out if it had any fruit. When he reached it, he found nothing but leaves, because it was not the season for figs. Then he said to the tree, "May no one ever eat fruit from you again." And his disciples heard him say it.

Now when reading this, it probably sends a couple of red flags of curiosity. First, why would Jesus be expecting fruit from this tree even when it wasn't "due season" for fruit yet? Second, why would he curse the tree when it wasn't time for it to produce in the first place? The answer to both of those questions is simple . . . because Jesus expected the fruit to be there based on his faith and not the physical situation. Some may argue that in this text, he did not know if fruit was on it or not, so he was just going to see. My rebuttal is the fact that Jesus being both God and man was the smartest walking human on the planet; he knew that it was not time for figs yet, but he still expected fruit based on his own faith. I mean, if he knew that the woman by the well was living with a man she was not married to, then he knew whether this tree had fruit, or not. Therefore, I believe that, at times, our faith can mandate a manifestation on demand.

However, there is a caveat here that I do not hear in most popular teachings. Faith can only dictate time when it agrees with God's will. This has been my common theme in this book because I want people to understand that all roads in our faith life must lead back to God the Father. I continue to point to Scriptures like Isaiah 55:11, because we must understand that God's Word will only accomplish what he wants. To the naked eye, the story of Jesus and the fig tree may look like his words held the power to kill the tree and render it fruitless. I would argue that it was his faith behind his Words that did this work. Remember, the Lord is not going to expect anything from us that he wouldn't do himself, and he expects our words and actions to *show* what's in our hearts.

Some may still ask if it's possible for our faith to dictate the time of our manifestation before its "due?" Let me try a different approach and answer that question with another: "If doubt and fear can dictate time, why can't our faith?" Say there is a twenty-year-old man who is not "due" to die until he is eighty-five years old. This young man doubts anyone loves him and is fearful that no one will ever care for him, so he kills himself. It is safe to say that doubt and fear dictated the time of his death and brought it into manifestation long before it was "due." Remember fear and faith are identical twins: faith is the confident assurance that what is hoped for will happen, while fear is the confident assurance that what we are afraid of will happen. The only thing separating these two siblings is one is hope and the other is being afraid. Also keep in mind, we are called to faith, to have a hope in a good life while here on earth and a beautiful eternity with God because of his son Jesus Christ. Furthermore, 1 John 5:4 says that *"everyone born of God conquers or is victorious over the world."* The word *"world"* here means its affairs and things of the earth . . . *time* is a thing of the earth, right? Also, look at other miracles in the Word like healings or being raised from the dead. According to the "world's" timing, the person was not supposed to get better until later, or not at all, yet faith made it happen. Multiple times Jesus told people, "*According to your faith . . . ,*" when they received their breakthroughs. He didn't say "according to the world's time." The miracle was totally contingent on the person's faith; a faith that coincides with the Lord's will. Again, this shows me that *some* things are readily available to us and ready to manifest, when we want them, as long as these desires run alongside his plan, regardless of the world's will.

After considering my last point about faith and how it can trump our physical conditions at times, I want to shift gears a bit to share some other reasons we should stay in the Word of God daily to grow our faith. This school of thought is vital, and I have stressed the importance of Scripture to address this issue.

While waiting on the breakthrough that would ultimately inspire this book, I fell into a dry season, like most people experience. Some call these seasons, "the wait." I already did a deep dive into this topic, but here I want to discuss the effects a dry season can have. The time when it feels like absolutely nothing is happening, and we start to wonder if God is even listening, or if he even cares. During my wait for the job I wanted, the Lord gave me a dream one night along with a warning. This dream was a perfect representation of what I was going through at that point in my faith life. If I am being honest, it was more of a mental picture that kept popping up in my mind and heart. I saw a nice refreshing above ground swimming pool that was full of cool crystal-clear water on a blazing hot summer day. This pool was full to the brim and had pool toys in it.

As some time went by, the sun got higher in the sky, and the outside temperature rose even higher. The water began to evaporate, and the pool was only half full.

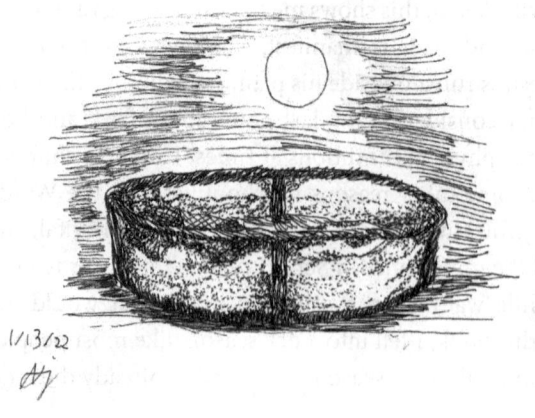

Finally, with no fresh water being put in the pool, the water evaporated all the way down to only an inch left.

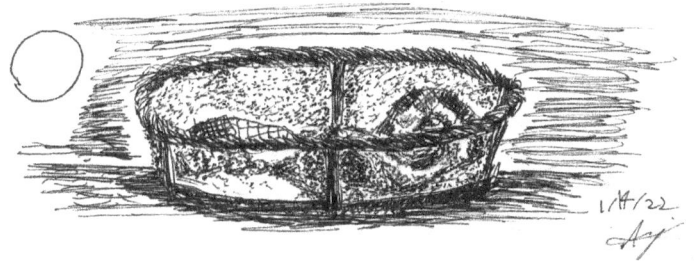

After this dream, the Lord helped me see that the pool represented my heart, the water represented my faith over the situation and the sun represented the enemy and his attacks. I will talk more about how Satan assaults our faith in a later chapter but here I want to use this imagery to highlight our faith's total dependency on the Word of God.

Jesus said in John 4:14, *"But those who drink the water I give will never be thirsty again. It becomes a fresh, bubbling spring within them, giving them eternal life."* The water of Jesus is the Word of God, among other things, and when we stay connected to his Word, we are refreshed. Jesus also said in the Gospels that he is the vine, and we are the branches, and we will bear much fruit when we remain in him. When thinking about this from a simple botany level, it makes perfect sense because the vines of a plant are its veins and through its veins flow the nourishment needed to keep the whole plant alive. When the other parts of the plant are disconnected from the vines, the plant dies. At the end of his vine analogy, Jesus said "*. . . apart from me you can do nothing.*" The heat from the attacks of the enemy will be inevitable, brutal, hot and frequent, so if the *pool* of our heart is not continually filled with the water that is the Word of God, then the faith we have will begin to evaporate and dry until there is nothing left. I don't want to give the impression that I am talking about needing "new" faith or "bigger" faith. The Bible says all we need is a "mustard seed" of faith to do great things. Once we have purpose in our hearts to pursue something by faith, we do not need new faith; however, we do need to strengthen the faith we already have by staying in the Word daily to continue to replenish and refresh our faith.

One spring day while mowing my yard, I came across some balding spots where some grass blades had died, and I could see dirt. I looked up in frustration to see my neighbor's grass so deep and thick that it looked like it would need a saw to cut a square out. Then I did research about how to get my yard to grow like that, and I came across an interesting article. The writer said to look at a yard as if it were the Amazon Forest. The author then said that just like the Amazon is full of millions of trees, your yard is a forest full of millions of grass blades. In the Amazon, when a tree falls and dies off, it leaves seeds so another tree will take its place. Our lawns differ in this aspect because when grass blades fall and die, they do not leave seedlings to replace it, so the seed must be placed. This is called "overseeding" and must be done every fall and spring to get that deep thick grass we all want.

Then the Lord used this simple everyday example to show me the importance of overseeding our hearts with the seeds of faith. Just like in the pool analogy, the seeds of faith that are put into our hearts can dry up, get lost, destroyed, and even stolen. To prevent our hearts from developing bald spots like my lawn, we must stay in the Word of God daily to overseed our hearts with faith. Jesus made this clear in Matthew with his parable about the Kingdom of God. He knew that life is messy, and at times, the seeds of faith sown in our hearts will get trampled over by others, fall in the rocky places we all have, and even stolen by the enemy. Consequently, the only way to replenish these lost seeds of faith is to get fresh ones from God's Word.

Building and maintaining our faith is also like house building a home. As I write this chapter, I am looking out my office window and can see a new home being finished across the street. Watching a home being built from a bare lot to a full finished home is a fascinating sight to see. Watching the homes in my area being built has helped me see a parallel between the home building process and the faith process. When looking at a home, there are many raw materials being used, and once the home is built, there are many utilities used to keep it functioning for years to come. At the base of every home is a big solid concrete slab called the foundation, and then there is the framework, wiring and so on. I see the same thing in our faith lives as shown in this list.

Concrete foundation	=	Our Salvation through Christ
Home Electricity	=	Joy
Home Lighting	=	Peace
Home A/C	=	Prosperity
	and so on…	

Look at this example through an allegorical point of view and not a literal one. The parts of the home only represent various ways we believe God gives to us in our faith lives, like joy, peace, and prosperity. With this image in our heads, I want us to see that every time we take in God's Word, we are building up a piece of our *"home"* of faith. We may read Scripture on joy at a time where everything is great in our lives, and there is no sadness. We may have all the money we need now with plenty to share, but still study what God says about prosperity. When we do this, we are building up and fortifying our home of faith. I think it's much easier to build a home when the weather is nice, and there are no elemental issues, versus when there is a hurricane outside. When was the last time you saw a construction crew building any sort of structure in bad weather? Same idea with our faith lives; it's much easier to have our faith built and strong during a calm season versus trying to build it up when we're right in the middle of a fight with the enemy. The only way to get, build and maintain our faith is through ingesting the Word of God. When we do this, we don't have to "get our faith ready" for expectation of miracles because we "stay ready" with this constant stream of God's Word.

Ingesting the Word should be one of our highest priorities. During studying, the Lord continued to reveal to me that I had wrong thinking when it came to 2 Corinthians 5:17. The Scripture reads, *"Faith comes by hearing and hearing by the word of God."* I thought that to be "really getting something" from the Bible, we had to block out hours of our day, sit down and read the Scriptures with our own eyes. If I was not doing Bible study this way, I had the feeling of wasting my time because I was not getting anything substantial from it. Looking back, I suppose I developed this thinking because I had a coach once who would pound in our heads that if we were not breathing hard or straining during practice, we were wasting time, or "if you ain't sweatin' then you ain't workin'," as he would put it. This thinking could not be further from the truth in working out or building faith. When it comes to the latter, the Lord showed me that the "hearing" he speaks of in the Scripture means just that, to hear. Explore the multiple ways to hear God's Word. Listen to the audio Bible, while cleaning the house or listen to a sermon on a topic that has been on your mind lately, while going for a walk. My personal favorite is having Scriptures play on my Bluetooth speaker all night as my family sleeps. Did you know that there are entire YouTube channels that have scriptures pertaining to various topics playing for hours with relaxing sound effects playing softly in the background? It's Awesome! The point is this, I do believe reading the Word is the best way to get it in our hearts and minds to "hear" God's Word. However, I now understand that we are all different, and what connects with me may not connect with another person, so there are multiple avenues to get his Word in our spirits, just like there are multiple ways to get essential vitamins into our physical bodies. The fact of the matter is that every time we ingest God's Holy Word, we are building our house of faith, brick by brick and beam by beam.

  I know there have been many concepts and viewpoints put forth in this chapter, as faith is one of the most powerful concepts within a Christian's life. There are many aspects of faith, so I want to be sure that this chapter shows what real faith is, the importance of it, its potential, where to get it and how to build and maintain it. Once again, people may say "No" to the requests we are believing, but if the desires agree with God's will for our lives, then what others say is irrelevant. We all may have missed out on some amazing things God had for us because we stopped at the first, second or tenth "*No*" from the world. That time is over dear friends; it's time to stand up and aggressively go after *all* God said we could have. Furthermore, those people who continue to say "*No*" to something when God said "Yes," may come to ruin on their way, if it's keeping us from what he has for us. I am not saying we should pray for terrible things to happen to someone who gets in the way between us and God's promises, but I am saying if they are doing so intentionally with evil in their hearts, the Lord will remove that obstacle, in whatever way he sees fit. This point deserves to be reiterated. We must adopt the attitude that no matter the situation, location, or any other condition, all God needs is our faith.

As I already talked about earlier, I took hold of this idea of faith as a young boy hearing other black people always talk about how white people "won't let them do this or that." And their attitude that because they are on food stamps, they can't aspire for higher things in life. However, as I read Scripture and learned from the Holy Spirit, I never once saw in any translation of the Bible that God's promises are constricted to ethnicity. Jesus did not say, "Anything you ask in my name, that will I do. [*Unless you are black.*]" I want you to hear me and hear me loud, do not let this world trick you into thinking you are a victim because of what you look like. We are only victims when we allow ourselves to be. Remember that if each of us is a child of God, then no weapon, of the physical or spirit, will work against us. As long as we have faith in God and his Word, nothing will overtake us. Hold this concept in your minds and really think about it. *Live*, *Walk* and *Fight*. Remember that a Christian is commanded to:

- Live by faith -Habakkuk 10:38
- Walk by faith -2 Corinthians 5:7
- Fight the good fight of faith -1 Timothy 6:12

If we are told to live, walk, and fight in faith, how can we do that if we do not go to the only place to get faith, God's Word? Remember, ingesting the Holy Word of God daily is not for his benefit, but for ours to get and cultivate this powerful faith he has given us. This faith is very precious to God, but it's repulsive and dangerous to the enemy, which is why he attacks it with such voracity.

Always remember that the only way we can relentlessly, full bore chase down the promises of God with our ears pinned back is if we have real faith in the Lord and his promises. We must be fully convinced and believe. It's just like a trapeze artist, they do these death defying stunts at crazy heights because they know there is a safety net to catch them, if they fall. The same is true in our faith life: The Lord and his faithfulness is our safety net, as long as we are pursuing the Kingdom and all that entails. Exactly as it says in Psalm 121:3 NIV, *"He will not let you slip–he who watches over you will not slumber."*

Under Attack

As the old saying goes, "There are two things that are inevitable in life. Death and taxes." I want to add a third to that list, attack from the enemy. Some people don't like to mix words like fighting or war with Jesus and the Christian faith, but those people obviously do not read the Bible with understanding of this issue. If they did, they would know God is a warring God along with being a loving Father. As anyone who has been a Christian for long can tell, from the moment we first pray for something, a fight to keep our faith will come. Let's take a step closer and analyze a few concepts. First, why does the attack come? Second, when does it come, and third, what do we do when the attack comes?

Why Does the Attack Come?

For starters, the attack comes in our lives because Satan absolutely hates us, and he wants to turn our faith into fear. Satan's job is to *wear out* the saints according to Daniel 7:25. We may experience an attack at work. The enemy is not after us or our jobs; what would the Devil do with our jobs? He is not after our kids or our spouses either. He is after our faith because if he can poison the well of our hearts, then he can kill a whole generation of faith. Remember when I mentioned that faith and fear are siblings? The Devil wants to pull the "ole switcheroo," take our faith in God's Word, and in its place put his fear and doubt. His game plan is simple, and it's written plain as day in the Book of John when Jesus said that the enemy comes to *"steal, kill and destroy."* The Bible gives us insight to the Devil's game plan in First Peter when the verse likens Satan to " . . . *a roaring lion 'looking' for someone to devour."* The good news is that this verse tells us the enemy can't just go around eating anyone he wants. The main point is the enemy not only attacks because he hates us, but because he wants what is in our hands. He wants our faith because he knows faith is the key that unlocks the miraculous in our lives.

Look at the story in chapter one of Job; the real reason Job went through his trials is revealed. I have heard for years people use this story to talk about how God will sometimes bring hardship to our lives to somehow "strengthen our faith." I do not buy this idea for a second. It is true that tests come to purify our faith and show it to be genuine. Our faith must stand trial, and as a matter of fact, James 1:3 guarantees it when it says in the Amplified Bible version,

> *Consider it nothing but joy, my brothers and sisters, whenever you fall into various trials. Be assured that the testing of your faith [through experience] produces endurance [leading to spiritual maturity, and inner peace]. And let endurance have its perfect result and do a thorough work, so that you may be perfect and completely developed [in your faith], lacking in nothing.*

However, I submit that there is a vast difference between a test and an attack. The Lord showed me a long time ago that a test from him does not come to kill us, it comes to grow us. Sometimes God wants to see if we truly believe him, much like a football coach scheduling tough games in the preseason to expose the weaknesses his team may have and to strengthen them for their conference games. The coach does not do this because he wants his team to suffer and lose but allows this tougher opponent to grow his squad.

Another way to look at the difference between attacks and tests is the results that come out of the experience when it's over. The test comes with an objective to draw something out of us or to instill something in us. For example, return to the story of my new career. While I went through the trials waiting for the job to manifest, a multitude of blessings came as a result, including the job itself. The best of all blessings was the wisdom and insight that is the subject matter of this book. While waiting, I sat at God's feet, prayed, and learned, while I saw the Bible unfold like a beautiful map leading me to where I am now. An attack has no purpose other than to torment, so I do not believe attacks come from the Lord because the Bible makes it clear he is passionate about us, and he is a caring Father. I am a father, and I could not ever imagine bringing calamity into my kids' lives to teach them lessons or make them stronger. Earlier in the book I talked about the "wills" of the Lord, and his sovereignty. Please always remember that God's thoughts toward us are of good and not of evil. It was not God's "will" that a 5-year-old was shot and killed in a drive by last week or for a family to go bankrupt after the father lost his job due to COVID-19. We must not ever allow anyone to use God's sovereign power as a rationale to understand when evil happens in our lives by seeing him as a mean, all-powerful God on a throne who will decide at the drop of a hat if good or bad comes our way. God is always good! Always, and his plans for us are of good and *not* of evil. We have someone else to blame for all the pain in the world; his name is Satan, and he is the father of all fear, sin and lies.

In Mark 1:41, the Bible records an interaction between a leper and Jesus, when the ill man came to the Lord asking if he would heal him. Many versions just say that Jesus was, *"moved with compassion"*; however, I like the NIV version when it says Jesus was *"indignant."* The word "indignant" means, "Feeling or showing anger or annoyance at what is perceived as unfair treatment." Jesus was not annoyed with the man for asking for help, he was feeling anger that the man was sick in the first place and was experiencing this unfair treatment of the enemy. With Scriptures like these throughout the Bible, it is logical to conclude that attacks, pain, and disaster do not come from the Most-High God or his son Christ Jesus.

I offer a different view on the hardships of Job from chapter one, verse five. In the Amplified Bible version, which says:

> *When the days of their feasting were over, Job would send [for them] and consecrate them, rising early in the morning and offering burnt offerings according to the number of them all; for Job said, 'It may be that my sons have sinned and cursed God in their hearts.' Job did this at all [such] times.*

It's very important to note the end of the verse when it claims that Job said, *"It may be that my sons have sinned . . . "* This supports the thought that all the sacrifices and holy activities Job did, although good on the surface, were done out of fear for his kids. This action done out of fear sets up the chain of events that makes Job famous. Another key thing to note of the interaction between God and Satan, while they are discussing Job, proves my view at the beginning of this chapter that God does not attack us. Job 1:11–12 solidifies this idea when Satan tells God:

> *But put forth your hand now and touch (destroy) all that he has, and he will surely curse you to Your face.*

God did not do what the Devil asks; God did not hurt Job at all; however, God revealed Satan in the next verse:

> *Behold, all that Job has is in your power, only do not put your hand on the man himself.*

Now before getting into this point, I think it's worth the effort here to show this as another example of a common theme I have shared throughout this book. God is a good God, and his plans for us are good and not evil. Remember, the Bible never contradicts itself but always compliments itself. Some people believe the school of thought that God causes bad to happen to teach us something. In the book of Jeremiah, God claims to have good plans toward us, but then in Job if in fact he places us in the evil one's hands sometimes, that would be a massive contradiction. I think it's safe to say that would be an evil thing to do, right?! This then makes Job 1:11 most intriguing because it seems that the Lord was telling Satan, *"Behold (look) that he is 'already' in your hands because of what he has been doing."* Remember Job had been sacrificing to God out of *fear* that his kids did something sinful. Therefore, I believe that

Job's fear, and *not* God, placed what he had in the enemy's hands in an effort to "teach" Job something. There is a reason we are told over 300 times in the Bible to *"fear not,"* and it's because when we do fear, we place ourselves and what we have in the enemy's hands.

One day, Holy Spirit revealed to me that at the heart of every single fear we have is a lie. This is the reason that Satan is called the "Father of Lies." If he can get us to believe a lie, then he can keep us in fear. He won't come at us with fear first, and then try to get us to believe a lie. We are not going to be afraid of something we know isn't true. However, if he can get us to believe a lie, then fear can torment us because we believe what we hear, see or experience is true. God is such a Champion of Truth, and the enemy hates it because there is freedom in truth, as John 8:32 says, *". . . and your freedom in all areas is what Jesus paid for with his blood."* When it comes to the attack of Satan in our lives, we can be prepared. Even though he is a ferocious enemy, he is a predictable one, as well.

When Will the Attack Come?

The second of the three questions is "When will the attack come?" There is no 100% sure answer for this one but there are some strong patterns that the enemy follows. I love to go fishing, and it's funny how the Lord can use any activity to show us something. Let me give a crash course into the world of bass fishing to give this story context. When bass fishing to catch the biggest fish, a person has to go during prime seasons of the year. For this fish in particular, the best season for the fattest fish is during the pre-spawn, when the females feed and eat as much as they can in preparation for the spawn. Then the fisherman has to pair that timing with the right lure to use. The Lord showed me that the enemy takes this same tact with us. He knows the best time to attack and tempt us. Furthermore, he knows what bait to use and how to use it. This is one reason that the Bible calls him an *"opportune hunter."*

When looking at the temptation of Jesus Christ recorded in Matthew, we see the enemy use this strategy. The Bible talks about Jesus resisting the enemy and telling him to leave. The Devil did leave until a *more opportune time*. This prompted me to ask what is the *"opportune time"* for the attack, the punch, the persecution, the arrow?

Right Before:

I learned that the temptation came right before Jesus began his public ministry. Matthew 4:1–11 depicts the temptation, then verse 12 starts with Jesus beginning his ministry, so literally the attack came right before the miracles and healings start, the disciples' group was formed, and the Gospel was preached. I am convinced from Scripture and from personal experience that one of the enemy's opportune times is right before a breakthrough. Why would the enemy pick this time to attack the Lord? Granted, it was a time when Jesus was tired, hungry, and weak physically. The Devil came at the end of the fast. Like a lion, the enemy will not attack when we are strong, alert, and able to fend him off. No, he wants an easy meal. Consequently, there is more to his strategy. I think the enemy attacked at that point in time because it was his last opportunity to kill the seed of faith that would spark a movement in the world that would win untold billions to the Lord.

Right After:

Another opportune time that attack comes is right after God sows something in our hearts, and the seed is fresh. Again, looking at the temptation of our Lord, it is no coincidence the story of the temptation is sandwiched between two very important events in Jesus' earthly life. Not only was it right before he began his ministry, but the Bible shows an attack happened right after Jesus' baptism in Matthew 3:11. During his baptism, Jesus came out of the water, and the dove of the Holy Spirit came out of heaven and rested on him, empowering him to begin his ministry, as told in Matthew 4:12. Then an audible voice that everyone heard said, *"This is my* son *in whom I am well pleased."* This was not some quiet telepathic whisper that everyone *heard* in their hearts. This was the loud powerful voice of God confirming Jesus. Right after this powerful seed had been placed in the heart of Jesus, the enemy's attack came. This is by design; remember the enemy's plan; he wants to steal, kill, and destroy. In this instance, the enemy was trying to steal that fresh seed of faith placed in Jesus at his baptism. If Satan had succeeded, then the precious seed of faith would have been destroyed that was in the hearts of the people who witnessed the baptism.

When Weak, Alone, Lazy:

This timing of attack seems obvious. A predator does not attack the prey when the prey is strong, surrounded by help and able to fight off an attack. Satan, the predator to our souls, attacks the same way. Continue looking at the temptation of Jesus found in Matthew chapter four. Jesus had not eaten for forty days, that's 960 hours, folks. I think it's safe to say that Jesus was probably physically weak, tired, and maybe a smidge grumpy! It is scientifically proven that when the body is deprived of nutrients, it can't think straight or function correctly. This is why Scripture puts a premium on taking care of our physical health, as well as our spiritual health.

Also, Jesus was alone at that time. This was a big idea for me to understand because I am a "loner," and I like to be alone when I can. Every Animal Planet documentary that I have seen shows the predator singling out the tired, weak one in the groups. When we are alone, we have no physical and emotional support or help. The concept of accountability partners comes into play here, I believe this is why the Bible tells us to pray fervently for each other.

In our laziness is another perfect time for the enemy to strike. From experience, I know that the attack comes when I am lazy in my faith. This is another reason for the importance of staying in the Word of God. I am convinced the enemy wants to lull us into laziness and pride. After we receive manifestation from the Lord, it is easy to think, well *I got it now, so I don't need God for anything else for a moment.* We put our faith away, sitting on a shelf to be used on an "as needed basis." Or even worse, we do not expect an attack. Many Christians go through life thinking that the Devil is some cute little, red-horned Count Dracula type of dude who may cause some mischief here and there, but nothing major. I have talked to folks that think evil is not even real. These people are easy snacks for the kingdom of darkness. When I was a kid, I heard my pastor say, "The greatest trick the Devil ever pulled was convincing the world he does not exist." If he can convince people that he does not exist or will not attack, then there will be no defense to fight. Friends, this is dangerous because it is the equivalent of putting our weapons away and letting them collect dust. Remember, we are instructed to live by faith and fight the fight of faith every day, while expecting the enemy to throw his punches and shoot those fiery arrows.

It's important to realize that this is not a conclusive list of times the enemy will attack. There are some nuances that are specific to each person. The enemy could use the bait of lust to kill the manifestation some people want in their lives. He may come at a time when a couple just got into a big fight, and the girl at work who flirts with the guy is wearing bright red lipstick, which happens to be his favorite color, and she starts sending him signals that she wants him. Or many people may have drug addictions, and every time they get stressed out, they use it. It just may happen one day when we might be at our weakest that we get fired and have no idea how to pay the bills; and guess what's coming our way friends, the opportune hunter Satan is coming full force, and he is wise. He knows he will not get the desired result if he attacks the man who struggles with lust by coming at him the same way he would attack the people who struggle with drugs. Satan and his kingdom have been around for a long time, and he knows the Bible says for us to be vigilant, which means to keep careful watch for possible danger or difficulties.

UNDER ATTACK

What To Do When an Attack Comes?

There are a multitude of ways we can and should respond when an attack from the enemy comes our way. I want to highlight the most important actions we can take.

Get Protection and Help:

We have to protect ourselves. Remember in the chapter on prayer I talked about how we pray for safety and strength. Believers, we already have divine protection, as Psalms 91 tells us that God covers us with his wings. But having protection and asking to use it when needed are two different things. I like to be alone, and I talked about how the enemy can use that to his advantage to attack. Alongside the "loner" mentality can also come pride. I struggle with the issue that I always try to accomplish things on my own. This quality has some merit, but it can morph into a *"well, I can fight off this temptation or issue alone, too"* kind of thinking within myself, and I continue without invoking God's help or protection. James 4:7 says, *"Submit yourselves, then, to God. Resist the devil, and he will flee from you."* The first part of this Scripture outright destroys the thinking some, like me, may have when we try to "resist" on our own. Notice that before we can even think about resisting the enemy, we must first submit to the Lord. This is no coincidence. It must happen like this, again, we have to go to the One who already did what we are trying to do. If we want to learn how to become a millionaire, we go to a person who is already a millionaire. If we want a forty plus year happy marriage, then we go to a couple who has been together at least that long. Use the same idea with resisting the attacks of the enemy: we want to withstand the attack and win, then we have to turn and submit our entire selves to the One who already faced the same attacks, and he won . . . Christ Jesus. The writer in Psalm 11:2 boldly says, *"My help cometh from the LORD, which made heaven and earth,"* Then again in Psalm 46:1, Scripture promises us, *"God is our refuge and strength, a very present help in trouble."* *"Very present"* can also be translated as *"immediate."* There is no room, and no time, for being a lone wolf trying to navigate this life and defeat the enemy on our own. We have a loving Father in heaven and a strong champion in Jesus who already won; we just have to ask and use the help he offers.

Another thing to do while getting protection during an attack of our faith is to call on that same faith. I just talked about faith from the aspect of it being our currency in the spiritual to receive God's promises in our lives, and now I want to talk about faith as a defense mechanism. When talking about our daily living, the writer in Ephesians 6 tells us to put on the full armor of God. Part of that armor is the shield of faith; now why would faith be a shield? Simple, when considering what a shield does, its sole purpose is to protect the person wielding it. In the case of the Christian, the shield of faith protects from the fiery arrows of the enemy: Arrows of doubt, pain, and lies that look true. When the volley of arrows come from the enemy's camp to attack, we lift the shield of our faith in God's Word to block it. For example, imagine we are believing God for healing in our bodies, but we still have physical pain in that area, so the enemy fires his bolt of *"see you are not healed and never will be."* We lift up our shields of faith, standing on scriptures like Isaiah 53:5 and say, *"by* his *stripes I am healed."* Maybe we have a situation where we have asked the Lord for wisdom about an issue, and we believe he has shown us the truth and its good news. Then the Devil fires at us saying, *"That can't be true because you do not deserve good news . . . look what you did."* In that instance, we throw up our shields as in James 1:5 and say, *"the Lord said he loves to help when I lack wisdom and he promised that I would get his help as long as I don't, so I do not doubt, Satan!"* See my friends, wait . . . shhh, can you hear that? If we are quiet, then we can hear those arrows being extinguished while they hit those faith shields! *Thonk, Thonk!* We also fight back by using our swords. The Word of God is like that of a sword. We lift up our shield of faith in what God said about the issue, and then we hit back with the sword of the Spirit, which gives even more promises from God. Here is an example:

Under Attack

Imagine you are in real need of a job, a great paying job with all the benefits, but the job market and all the news seems bad. No one is hiring, so the enemy attacks your faith that God will provide. In that case, you lift the shield of faith as in Scriptures like Philippians 4:19, *"God will supply all my need"* to block those fire arrows and attack with the sword of the Spirit with Scriptures like Psalm 37:25, *"I have never seen the righteous forsaken or their children begging for bread."* We can trust our faith in the Lord to help and protect us from the enemy's attacks.

Keep Focus:

Focus is key in every aspect of life, no matter what we are doing. Whether studying for a test or lifting weights, pretty much all we do in life demands our focus. There is no difference in our spiritual lives, especially spiritual warfare. I received a major revelation about this topic while waiting for that same job that I have talked about multiple times. I will never forget, while reading the Bible one night at the youth center, I did a deep dive on the story of Peter walking on water. Most of us know the story well, and I have already used the story for other points, but it's so full of knowledge that it deserves to be revisited. Most would say Peter began to sink when he lost faith in Jesus' ability to keep him safe, which may be true, but what caused Peter to lose his faith? Keep in mind that before Peter began to sink, he was already out on the water a good way from the boat. He didn't sink as soon as he stepped out of the boat. When we read the story, it says in verse thirty, *"But when he saw the wind, he was afraid and, beginning to sink, cried out, 'Lord, save me!'"* Did you catch that? *"But when he saw"* the conditions surrounding him, he lost his faith. In order to see something, we have to be looking at it, and in Peter's case, he took his focus *off* Jesus who was telling him to come, and he started looking *on* the conditions surrounding him. How many times have we done this in our lives? How many times has God told us to "come" but we lost focus on him and his Word and looked at the surrounding conditions? Ecclesiastes bluntly tells us, *"He that observeth the wind shall not sow; and he that regardeth the clouds shall not reap."* If we observe the conditions and not God's promises, we run the risk of not seeing manifestation. With a bit of a disclaimer, I am not advocating that we don't acknowledge the facts of our conditions, but I am saying that these facts do not overrule the truth, which are the holy promises of God. If anyone is sick, please continue to see doctors, take medicine, and make healthy choices until healing comes. If anyone is lonely and wants a spouse, continue to live a godly single life, and do not live with anyone until married on the wedding day. All these examples show when we take our focus off Jesus and give it over to the conditions . . . we will sink.

The result of keeping our focus on Jesus will be perfect peace. Keeping our focus on him also means to stay focused on his Word. The King James version of Isaiah 26:3 says, "*You will keep him in perfect peace, whose mind is stayed on you, because he trusts in you.*" Notice this promise of peace comes with a stipulation. To experience this perfect peace of God, our minds must be on him and his Word. If we allow our minds to go to other things, like the conditions surrounding the situation, then we cannot expect this perfect peace. Also, it is very important to note in this Scripture that we can *only* keep our mind on God, if we trust him. The tail end of the Scripture says, " . . . *whose mind is stayed on you, because he trusts in you."* Notice the parallel there. Our mind is stayed on God, *because* we trust him. If we don't trust the Lord, then we will not focus on him and as a result perfect peace is not present. I submit that we often focus on what we trust, and in a physical world, it is very easy to only trust what we can see, i.e., the conditions. Again, this is why the Bible tells us to walk by faith and not by sight. This idea ties back to the importance of staying in the Word. When we do this, we can boldly declare to the enemy during his onslaught, "*Satan! Because I trust the Lord, my mind is on* him, *therefore he will keep my mind at perfect peace!"*

Under Attack

Get Tough:

Lastly, we have to get tough, which means we have to fight. Remember, I talked about this Christian life as being a fight, and I don't mean a nice, clean, honorable boxing match. The enemy we face wants to steal our peace, kill our faith, and destroy our future. Obviously, I mean that we fight in the spirit through prayer and faith in the Scripture, but I also suggest we fight with attitude. The best way to fight with an attitude is to set it in our hearts that we are going to believe and trust God, no matter what. We must get tough and adopt the mindset of Shadrach, Meshach and Abednego in Daniel 3:18 when they told the king to his face, *"But even if he* [God] *does not, we want you to know, Your Majesty, that we will not serve your gods or worship the image of gold you have set up,"* in response to God saving them from the furnace since they refused to kneel to false Gods. I call that *"even if he doesn't"* type of faith. When we have that kind of attitude, the type that makes all of hell shudder, the enemy cannot touch us then. This kind of thinking is what makes faith so detestable to the enemy because it's the kind of faith he cannot destroy.

Remember, we fight with our mouths. I have already talked about the power of our mouths, but here I want to specifically talk about the power of praise in our mouths. Psalm 8:2 KJV is awesome because it says, *"Out of the mouth of babes and sucklings hast thou ordained strength because of thine enemies, that thou mightest still the enemy and the avenger."* Other translations say, *"from the praise of babes,"* and here in the King James version, the word *still* is the Hebrew word *šāḇaṯ* and means "cause (make) to fail."[1] We are the children of the Almighty, we are his *"babes and sucklings."* When we restructure this Scripture, it is saying, *"Out of the mouth (praise) of God's children, he has ordained strength because of the enemy, that thou mightest cause what the enemy and avenger is trying to do to fail."* Scripture is telling us that when we praise him and open our mouths it causes what the enemy is trying to do in our lives to fail. Again, what is the enemy trying to do? What is his

---

1. H7673 - Šāḇaṯ - Strong's Hebrew

game plan? To steal, kill and destroy us and our faith. But when we praise the Lord, and all his goodness, that dog won't hunt with the Lord, and the enemy will lose!

The other aspect of being tough is knowing our rights. Think of it this way, say a person does not know her rights as a property owner. She comes home from vacation one day to find a home full of people squatting on and in her property. She turns the corner of the street and sees her beautiful lawn destroyed. On one side someone dug a hole in the Bermuda grass lawn to create a fire pit, and on the other side, there is someone dropping their pants to relieve themselves. She goes inside and sees all personal belongings defaced or stolen, her kids' rooms destroyed and three filthy people in her bed. Now imagine she sees all this in front of her and does absolutely nothing about it, gets back in her car and leaves because she is ignorant of her rights. That's crazy, isn't it? No one in their right mind would leave property and people there like that. Realize, friends, that many of us do allow similar scenarios in our spiritual lives.

Jesus said in Luke 10:19, "*Behold, I give unto you power to tread on serpents and scorpions, and over all the power of the enemy: and nothing shall by any means hurt you.*" Breaking this down, the first use of power in the Greek is *exousia* and means "*force, authority or jurisdiction.*"[2] The second use of power in this verse is *dynamis* in the Greek and means "*work, power or influence.*"[3] Rewording the Scripture using its original meaning, it says, "*Behold, I have given you (force, authority or jurisdiction) over all the (work, authority or jurisdiction) of the enemy.*" See how powerful this is? We have this authority because Jesus gave it to us. He received this authority when he obeyed God and became our sacrifice. Consequently, defeating sin and Satan, then he was given the Name above all names, so everything must fall to his authority, whether they like it or not. However, the enemy knows this, and I believe that if he cannot accomplish plan A (stealing, killing, and destroying us), then he goes to plan B (wanting us ignorant and weak.)

2. G1849 - Exousia - Strong's Greek
3. G1411 - Dynamis - Strong's Greek

Under Attack

Ignorant of our rights and authority as believers, because he knows that if we come into the knowledge of what is ours, then we will get tough and won't put up with his attacks.

Look back at the example about having squatters on a property. However, this time the woman knows her rights and authority. While driving down the street, she sees what I described earlier. It's going to be a vastly different reaction. If it were me, I likely wouldn't even stop the car to get out. I would probably do some Batman window jump move and start getting after folks.

I continue to stress the importance of staying in the Lord, his Word and prayer because all he said we can do, be and have is there for us to seek and receive. God only knows how much the enemy has already stolen from all of us with his lies, fear, and attacks. However, there is an old song that we used to sing at church in the 1990s when I was a boy that tells this truth. The chorus is *"I went to the enemy's camp, and I took back what he stole from me."* [4] From this point on friends, I want us to get tough when the enemy attacks and do just what the song said, *"take back what he stole from you!"*

We not only have to get tough in what we say and how we act, but also in our thinking. When we get tough on something, we make it do what we want it to. Sometimes as a father, I have to get tough on my girls to make them do what I know is best for them. Remember when I talked about guarding our hearts when it comes to invasive thoughts that want to come in and sow seeds of fear and doubt? Sometimes this happens, because we are human after all, and these thoughts get in and start to do their work of dislodging us from our faith. When this happens, we have to practice 2 Corinthians 10:5 when it says, *"Casting down imaginations, and every high thing that exalteth itself against the knowledge of God and bringing into captivity every thought to the obedience of Christ."*

We must make every imagination that tries to be higher against the knowledge of God, which is shown in the Bible, captive and force that thinking to obey Christ. If a thought comes in our minds that says we will not have our needs met and we will

---

4. *Enemy's Camp Lyrics*, lines 3–4.

struggle financially our whole lives, then those thoughts are now in violation of the Knowledge of God and must be brought down and forced to obey Christ. If the imaginations start to loom that our kids will never serve the Lord, and they will be lost despite raising them the way they should go, then that imagination has tried to exalt itself over what God said in Proverbs 22:6, so it must be cast down. We face a relentless merciless enemy, my friends. It's time we return the favor.

Then Comes the Prize

AT THE END OF every competition, at the conclusion of every fight, there is a champion. There is a clear winner and a prize to show that the struggle is over. Make no mistake about it, dear ones, we are in the fight of all fights every day: The fight of our faith. Remember faith cannot be seen, but it can be shown. How can something that is not seen have a prize to show when the fight is over and to reveal who won? What does our prize look like? The prize is specific to the person, so it depends on the individual. To the man dying of cancer, his prize may be the physical healing. To the woman battling alcoholism, her prize may be the physical strength to put her flesh in check and resist that temptation. The point is that no matter what we believe in God to give, the result our fight of faith will end in a conclusion at some point. I pray at the end, each one of us will be the victor holding that physical proof that God is faithful and that he fulfilled his promise.

Here is how the fight of faith happened for my sister and her husband. They have been married for over twenty-two years but had never conceived a child. The family prayed and believed with them for years that they would have a baby, but with each passing year, no baby came. Only my sister and God know how many tears she cried. Only she knows how many baby showers and empty Mothers' Days she endured while forcing a smile on her face for those around her, while looking in the mirror wondering what their child would look like. Only my brother-in-law knows how many times he voiced his desire to be a father while praying to the ultimate Father. All the while, they stood as a couple, and we stood as a family believing God based on the authority of his Word like Psalm 34 says. In the meantime, they became "parents" to other children as my brother-in-law works in a field that is entirely focused on youth. To some of those kids, he was the only Father figure they ever had and the only true Christian lifestyle they had ever seen. Especially from a man. My sister has a heart of compassion and love, being the glue to our family. She was the "mother" to many kids, and she showed countless young women how to live lives that please the Lord. As they showed their faith this way and continued to be faithful, God was working. Remember the Scripture says that even if a mother hen forgets her chicks, God does not forget us or his promises.

The prize of their faith was born on September 18, 2021, in the form of a healthy, happy baby boy named Mytchell. Now I am here to tell everyone that it is one thing to have the job we were believing God would give or living in the house we have pursued in faith, but it is an entirely different experience when the longing desire has a heartbeat. When every sound the miracle makes is a reminder of how good God is. Every day we see, feel, touch, and smell the promise come true. Where I'm from, we say, *"that hits a little different."* Throughout my book, I share "super Scripture sightings." These last few I found solidify the truth of the goodness of God.

"God will not leave, nor forsake, give you up or let you down (Hebrews 13:5 AMP), *because* our faith is far more precious than Gold (1 Peter 1:7)."

"Those who wait (expect) for the Lord will gain new strength; they will mount up with wings like eagles, they will run and not get tired, they will walk and not become weary (Isaiah 40:31). *You will not get tired of waiting because you are waiting on the Lord, and he promised in Habakkuk 2:3 that He will not be late."*

Then Comes the Prize

"Those who trust in the Lord will not be disappointed in is expectation (Romans 10:11AMP) . . . *because* you have perfect peace since your mind is on him and you trust him (Isaiah 26:3-4)."

"If any man lacks wisdom, let him ask of God (James 1:5), *because* we cannot guide ourselves (Jeremiah 10:23)

After all this information, some readers may be wondering what to do next in our pursuit of God's promises for our lives. The number one thing we must do is make sure we are right with God by believing in and following Jesus. That he was God in the flesh, lived a sinless life and was the sacrifice for our sin. Then he rose again and is seated at the right hand of God, and he will return soon. Always remember that he did this, not out of obligation or necessity, but out of love. Exodus 34:14 in the Bible says that God is jealous after us. That word "jealous" there in the Hebrew is *qannā'* and means "*God does not bear any rival and avenger of departure from him.*"[1] That is not saying that God is a crazy boyfriend who will stalk us and kill us if we ever leave. On the contrary, it means that he wants back what is rightfully his, and that's us, you and me. We are rightfully his because he paid for us with the ultimate price. After that first and most important truth, the rest of the contents of this book tells how to pursue God's promises and obtain them in our lives.

By whatever path this book found its way into your hands, I am eternally grateful that each of you took time to read it. I pray that my experiences, concepts, and ideas bless and inspire, while pointing to the One who deserves all the praise, honor, and glory . . . Christ Jesus. I truly believe that this book will change the world because it will change someone's world. I pray that someone is you.

I called this book *Faith Hounds: A Relentless Pursuit* for this reason: Our lives are not only meant to be a pursuit of the promises of God, but also to be a relentless pursuit of the Father and his Kingdom. The good news is that unlike the fox evading the hound

---

[1]. H7067 - Qannā' – Strong's Hebrew

during a hunt, neither God nor his promises are running from us. God and his promises are ready and available to us, always.

Bibliography

Charis Meaning in Bible-New Testament Greek Lexicon-New American Standard. (2022). https://www.biblestudytools.com.

Enemy's Camp Lyrics. Brownsville Revival. 2022 Version. (2018). https://www.lyricsmode.com/lyrics/b/brownsville_revival/enemys_camp.html.

Evil English Definition and Meaning. Lexico Dictionaries. Oxford. (2019). https://www.lexico.com/en/definition/evil.

G1411 - Dynamis - Strong's Greek Lexicon (Kjv). (2022). https://www.blueletterbible.org/lexicon/g1411/kjv/tr/0-1/.

G1849 - Exousia - Strong's Greek Lexicon (Kjv). (2022). https://www.blueletterbible.org/lexicon/g1849/kjv/tr/0-1/.

H7673 - Šāḇaṯ - Strong's Hebrew Lexicon (Kjv). (2022). https://www.blueletterbible.org/lexicon/h7673/kjv/wlc/0-1/.

H2617 - Ḥeseḏ - Strong's Hebrew Lexicon (Kjv). (2022). https://www.blueletterbible.org/lexicon/h2617/kjv/wlc/0-1/.

H7067 - Qannā' - Strong's Hebrew Lexicon (Kjv). (2022). https://www.blueletterbible.org/lexicon/h7067/kjv/wlc/0-1/.

Huntsperger, Larry. *The Fisherman: A Novel.* Revell, 2003.

Martinez, Michael. "God Inhabits the Praises of His People." *Preacher's Notebook.* (July 31, 2021). https://www.preachersnotebook.org/god-inhabits-the-praises-of-his-people.

Peace English Definition and Meaning. Lexico Dictionaries. Oxford. (2022). https://www.lexico.com/en/definition/peace.

Phroureo Meaning in Bible-New Testament Greek Lexicon-New American Standard. (2022). https://www.biblestudytools.com.

Popovich, Steve. *The Greek Word for Confound, Make Ashamed and Disappoint: Kataischynō.* (2014). https://www.biblepopcorn.com/Trankataischuno.htm.

Simon, Paul, and Art Garfunkel. *The Sound of Silence.* New York City: Columbia Studios, 1964.

Virkler, Mark, and Charity Virkler Kayembe. *Hearing God through Your Dreams: Understanding the Language God Speaks at Night.* Shippensburg, Pa: Destiny Image, 2016.

Zeal English Definition and Meaning. Lexico Dictionaries. Oxford. (2021). https://www.lexico.com/en/definition/zeal.

www.ingramcontent.com/pod-product-compliance
Lightning Source LLC
Chambersburg PA
CBHW050827160426
43192CB00010B/1928